BOREALIS

An Isle Royale Potpourri

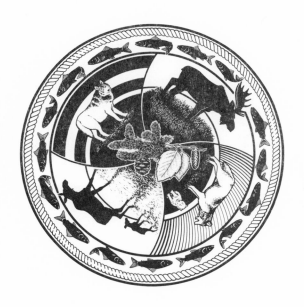

ISLE ROYALE NATURAL HISTORY ASSOCIATION
HOUGHTON, MICHIGAN

ISBN 0-935289-03-8

Compilation—Bruce Weber
Project coordinator—Gayle Pekkala
Editor—David Harmon
Introductions—Timothy Cochrane
Design—Christina Watkins
Cover illustration/Borealis symbol by
    Michael Taylor
Typography—TypeWorks
Printed by The Book Concern,
    Hancock, Michigan
Printed on recycled paper—
    Simpson Evergreen

Contents

Isle Royale

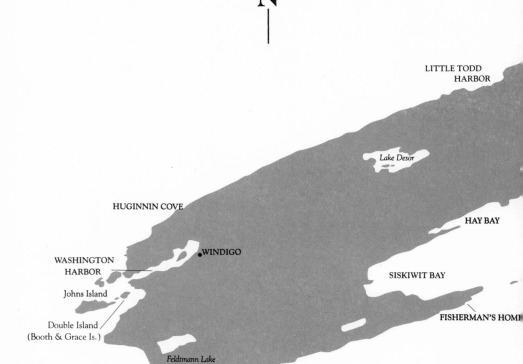

LITTLE TODD
HARBOR

Lake Desor

HUGINNIN COVE

HAY BAY

•WINDIGO

WASHINGTON
HARBOR

SISKIWIT BAY

Johns Island

Double Island
(Booth & Grace Is.)

FISHERMAN'S HOM

Feldtmann Lake

N

Blake Point

Belle Island (Fish Is.)

Scoville
Point

TOBIN HARBOR

SNUG HARBOR

Birch Island

McCARGOE COVE

ROCK HARBOR

DAISY FARM

Mott Island

ODD HARBOR

*Chickenbone
Lake*

Rock Harbor Lighthouse

Hatchet Lake

Lake Richie

Lake Whittlesey

CHIPPEWA HARBOR

Siskiwit Lake

MALONE BAY

L A K E   S U P E R I O R

Menagerie Island
Isle Royale Lighthouse

Crusading Conservationist: Ben East

INTRODUCTION - *Ben East's Island adventures and gifted pen stimulated interest in protecting Isle Royale. His articles awakened Michigan residents to the beauty of the Island. East consciously sought to create a mood of wonder and majesty that would provoke his readers to protect the Island under a national park designation. He understood the role the media could play in creating the park, and capitalized on events such as spiraling moose numbers and their eventual die-off, and his dangerous winter flight in 1930.*

East believed the park was a valuable antidote to downstate city life and the manipulation of the land in Midwestern farms. In his eyes, and in those of many that followed, the Island became an unspoiled refuge, despite its long and sweaty human history.

Ben East's campaign to help establish Isle Royale National Park was but one cherished effort in a distinguished career. As a crusading conservationist he was instrumental in the establishment of Tahquamenon Falls and Porcupine Mountains state parks. Born in 1898 in southeastern Michigan, East died on August 1, 1990. To recognize his instrumental role in protecting the Island, Isle Royale National Park named a staff dormitory in his honor at Rock Harbor.

In midafternoon on a July day in 1926 (I find it hard to believe it happened more than 50 years ago), *Patrol No. 1*, a motorship of the Michigan Department of Conservation, nosed cautiously around the treacherous twin reefs that guard the entrance to McCargoe's Cove, a narrow fjordlike arm of Lake Superior on the north shore of Isle Royale, and entered the long and beautiful harbor.

The patrol boat was some 35 feet long, not the much larger *No. 1* skip-

pered by Capt. Charles Allers for many years after 1930. In the charge of Capt.
Bob Ellsworth, a seasoned Great Lakes skipper, she was on her annual cruise
around Isle Royale, carrying a small party of state officials and guests of the
Conservation Department. I was aboard as a reporter and photographer for the
Grand Rapids Press, where I had worked as outdoor editor since the previous
April.

The bull moose, symbol of Isle Royale.

I had known from my country school days that Isle Royale was Michigan's
farthest north, a big but little-known island in Superior 50 miles off the mainland. All those years the place had tugged at my imagination. Now that I had
actually set foot on it, the first roadless wilderness I had ever seen, I was
finding it too wild, too untouched, too beautiful to be real.

No. 1 moved past Birch Island in the throat of the cove and dropped
anchor at the inner end, and as the afternoon waned our party settled down to
moose watching. The next few hours were the most exciting I had ever known.

The Chickenbone River, flowing out of Chickenbone Lake a mile in the interior of the Island, tumbled down a valley flanked by steep ridges and emptied lazily into the cove at its head. The shore around the stream mouth spread out in a wide marsh, with scattered clumps of alder and willow, and the moose of the vicinity had established a feeding ground and wallow there.

They came out of the timber one by one, bulls, cows, and one or two calves, until 12 or 15 were in sight within 100 yards of the patrol boat, feeding, wading knee-deep in the black muck of the marsh.

Years later my friend Ray Voss, the *Grand Rapids Herald* outdoor writer, would say, "There is something about a bull moose that makes him a lummox. With his flat antlers, overhanging snout, bell, and the hump on his back, he looks to me as if he had been built in sections by subcommittees with separate blueprints for a buffalo, a cow, and a camel, and then assembled by the general chairman after dark."

Ray was right, of course. But for all his lack of grace and beauty, there is also something majestic and imposing about this biggest member of the deer family. He wears his big palmated antlers with lordly pride, there is an impressive wildness about him, and I know no animal that speaks more eloquently of bogs and lonely lakes where man intrudes infrequently or not at all. That band at the mouth of the Chickenbone provided a spectacle I shall never forget.

Nothing could have been farther removed from the farmlands of southern Michigan where I had lived all my life than that wild, remote cove and its moose wallow. It was hard to believe that the place was part of the same state I called home.

We cruised around Isle Royale for the better part of a week, and I returned to the mainland awe-struck with its solitude and beauty. I did not realize it then, but I was entering into a love affair with an island, one that would endure for more than 50 years.

Over those years I have crossed Lake Superior more times than I can remember, in fair weather and foul and at all seasons, to visit the object of my affections. But of all the many trips I have made there, I remember none better than that first one in 1926, when I drank in the wild and heady enchantment of the place for the first time.

The big island is the top of a very ancient, worn-down mountain range, running southwest and northeast, roughly parallel to the Keweenaw Peninsula on the mainland of the Upper Peninsula. Varying in width from nine miles to a few yards, and 50 miles long, it has an area of 205 square miles, made up of long parallel ridges left by lava flows that poured from the depth of the earth eons ago.

The shore is broken and indented by bays and coves, narrow harbors, and winding channels. More than 200 outlying islands surround it, most of them toward the northeast end, varying in size from wave-washed bare rocks smaller than a house to Amygdaloid, a timbered sliver of rock close to five miles long.

Tucked away in the shallow valleys between the ridges are more than 30 lakes and too many bogs and ponds to count. Many of the lakes are small, but the biggest and deepest, Siskiwit, measures seven miles from end to end. Creeks and small rivers drain out of the lakes, some fast and brawling, some indolent and tranquil.

The Island rises highest at the southwest end, almost 800 feet above Superior, and slopes to the northeast where it ends in a series of long narrow points and rocky islets, with finger-like coves and bays between.

Save for bald open spots on the ridges, where there is little or no soil to cover the bare rock, it is timbered from shore to shore and end to end. There is maple and birch at the higher elevations, mostly balsam and spruce lower down, and around the lakes, mixed with birch and aspen. Scattered through the other timber is oak, cherry, pine, cedar, tamarack, and mountain ash. It's lovely forest, typical of the north country.

B ut lovely as it is, it accounts for hardly more than a small share of the Island's allure. It is the combination of gray rock and blue water, sparkling lakes and tumbling streams, sunlight and moonlight, storm and fog, the undergrowth and the carpet on the forest floor that make Isle Royale one of the most striking scenic wonderlands in the eastern half of this country.

The most abundant shrub in the understory is the thimbleberry, north-country member of the raspberry family, with very large leaves, white flowers, and tart scarlet fruit that yields a uniquely flavored jam prized over much of the Upper Peninsula. One of the most colorful bushes is the red-berried elder of the north, and in many places where the timber is open blueberries hang heavy with fruit.

The cool, wet summers and frequent fogs encourage the growth of moss and mushrooms. I have seen more varieties of moss and more areas carpeted with it on Isle Royale than in any other place I have visited, and during the frequent rains of September the ground is strewn with mushrooms as many-colored as the rainbow. One of the most attractive plants on the forest floor is the bunchberry, near kin to the flowering dogwood and a member of that same family, but growing only six inches tall. In May there are shaded places white with its blossoms, and in July they turn red with the fruit clusters.

The birds are typical of the northern wilderness. Seagulls around the harbors and nesting on some of the outlying islets; occasional eagles and ospreys over the lakes; a few great blue herons; loons on almost every lake, greeting the daybreak with their weird calling; ravens and crows; Canada jays, the friendly whiskeyjack of the north woods; the crow-sized pileated woodpecker; evening grosbeaks; and white-throated sparrows.

I have seen but one snake on the Island, a black or melanistic race of the garter snake. Only one other kind lives there, the midget red-bellied, rarely more than eight inches long, and it is not found often.

Two things the Island has that have given me some of the best days of my life: the moose herd and the pike fishing in the inland lakes. In the years when I visited the Island most frequently there were thriving populations of medium-sized pike in almost all of the 30-odd lakes.

There were no trails then save the well-worn moose trails, and for the human hiker they had two major drawbacks. They rarely went where he wanted to go, and a moose could step without difficulty over a fallen tree that a man had to detour around, no matter how thick the undergrowth. As a result, some of the lakes were hard to reach, and I never fished more than a handful of them. But that was enough. The fishing was something I'll never forget, both in those lakes and at the inner end of a few of the coves and harbors, especially where small streams came in, forming weedy shallows.

There was the day I carried a rubber raft in to Lake Livermore with a friend and neighbor from downstate Michigan, who was an enthusiastic pike fisherman but had never had spectacular luck with it. We portaged up a moose trail from the inner end of McCargoe's Cove to Chickenbone Lake, rowed across the two arms there, and portaged over a low ridge without even a moose trail, to the shore of Livermore.

I have always been willing to pay a fair price to see an unspoiled and untrod place, and Maurice and I paid it that day and more. We had only a small hand pump, and blowing the boat up with it was a major chore, so we inflated it in advance and carried it that way, as a canoe is portaged, using the

11

oars to make a neck yoke. The man under the boat looked like nothing so much as a yellow-backed (that was its color), two-legged beetle crawling up the ridges.

It had rained in the morning, and the sun had come out hot. We clawed through underbrush, stumbled over down timber, slipped on rocks, skirted beaver ponds. Where the trees were close together the man carrying the boat had to tip it up on one shoulder to get through, and all the way mosquitoes and blackflies kept us swarming company.

But five minutes after we floated the raft out on the lake and started casting along a section of shore strewn thick with downed treetops and snags, the effort and sweat and discomfort of the hike were wiped from our minds. Livermore was about as close to unfished water then as any place I have ever seen, and it's worth whatever it costs to lay a lure in such a lake as that.

I'd lay odds that no pike there had ever seen an artificial bait of any kind. So far as I had been able to find out in advance, nobody had laid a line over that water in a dozen years or more. The northerns were the untutored fish of wilderness lakes, unwary and reckless, ready to strike down and swallow anything that looked like fish smaller than themselves. Especially they liked our wobbling spoons, red-and-white, silver or copper, or white-and-black. The color did not seem to matter. The fake lures looked edible, the pike were hungry, they were plentiful enough that competition in the chow line was fierce. They behaved accordingly.

They were waiting in ambush around every downed treetop, beside every sunken log, in the shelter of every clump of weeds or lily pads. There were places where every cast meant a strike, and rarely did we make more than three or four casts without finding a fish willing to do business. In places they hunted down our spoons in packs.

They were of fair size, four to six pounds, but they were all whipcord and whalebone and not one of them failed to give us in full measure what we had come for. We did not keep count, but we must have brought between 30 and 40 to the boat in three hours of fishing. A few freed themselves in bucking lunges at the last minute. A few more that were hooked deep, we kept for the table. We eased the hooks out of the rest and slid them carefully back into the dark water of their home lake.

When our arms grew tired and the sun was dropping low, we went ashore and started the long hard hike back to our cruiser, moored at an old dock in McCargoe's Cove. For once in his life, Maurice had had all the pike fishing he wanted. For my part, I can recall no better day on a lake or steam anywhere I have fished.

It was the moose herd that made Isle Royale a camera hunter's dream place. The commonly accepted belief was that moose first appeared on the Island around 1912, crossing on the ice from Canada in a hard winter. But in the 1930s I had a letter from a man who had worked in the copper mines there around 1880, and he assured me that moose were abundant then. Authorities now believe they have lived on the Island, died out, and later returned a number of times in the unrecorded past.

When they began to show up after 1912, there was a fair herd of woodland caribou on the Island, but they dwindled rapidly after the moose appeared. The last sighting of a caribou I know about was in 1921, and they were extinct shortly after that. But as they faded out the moose prospered, until finally hard times came for them, too.

By the late 1920s leading wildlife authorities estimated that at least 1,000 moose were living in the Island's 205 square miles, and some estimates ran as high as 3,000. Certainly they were plentiful almost beyond belief.

On a hot day in July of 1930 I hiked, with Dick Lahti and Ellsworth St. Germain, then the Island game and fire warden, from Chippewa Harbor to Lake Richie, following worn moose trails. Richie was at that time as heavily used by moose as any lake on Isle Royale.

We reached it shortly after noon. Between then and sunset, when we started the hike out, I photographed more than 30 individual moose—bulls, cows, and calves. The hot weather and insect pests had driven most of the moose in that vicinity to seek relief in the water of the lake.

The high spot of the day came in midafternoon. Lahti and St. Germain and I decided on a dip to cool off. We stripped and were enjoying a welcome swim when Dick suddenly barked, "Look there," and pointed along the swamp-bordered shore.

Two full-grown cow moose had walked out of the cedars, 25 or 30 yards apart, and started to feed slowly toward one another in the shallow water along shore. Lahti must have suspected what was coming or he would not have alerted me.

I grabbed up the big cumbersome camera I relied on then for telephoto work and started on a run for the two moose, naked, partly screened by low brush that bordered the swamp. I still chuckle when I think of how I must have looked.

The cows were within 20 or 30 feet of each other, showing no sign of resentment, when their mood changed with abrupt suddenness. The hair on their necks lifted, their ears went back, and they rushed at each other like fighting stallions. They reared erect and flailed it out with their front legs, face to face. The blows were solid and the footwork was fast, sending water flying.

The fight lasted long enough for me to focus the big camera and make two of the rarest wildlife pictures I have taken, one of the two coming together in anger, the other of the slugfest that followed. One broke away in defeat and the other chased her and walloped her a final time on the behind for good measure.

That was the only time I have known or heard of cow moose brawling.

By the early 1930s the Isle Royale moose herd was in deep trouble. As has happened a number of times when big game animals are confined in a limited area, with neither hunting nor predators to hold their numbers in check, winter starvation overtook the herd with explosive suddenness.

Isle Royale was without timber wolves at that time. There was a plentiful population of coyotes, but they made no inroads on the moose, and the fast-growing herd had exhausted its cold-weather food supply. Balsam fir, the winter mainstay of the animals, was everywhere browsed as high as the biggest bulls could reach. The low-growing yew, commonly called ground hemlock, that had covered large areas with a dense evergreen tangle, was gone. Mountain ash trees had been stripped of their bark and girdled until there was hardly one remaining undamaged on the Island. A large-scale disaster was inevitable.

Holger Johnson, a commercial fisherman from Minnesota who summered on Isle Royale and had a comfortable log house at the entrance to Chippewa Harbor, elected in the fall of 1933 to winter over. Toward the end of winter he sent me by short-wave radio a report that moose were dying by the hundreds from hunger.

The Conservation Department realized it could not expect to save any large number of the animals, but it was not willing to stand back and let the herd dwindle, perhaps to extinction, without attempting some relief. On top of that, state game men had hopes of establishing a native moose population on the Upper Peninsula mainland. Before the summer of 1934 ended, a live-trapping and stocking project had been decided on.

In the fall Paul Hickie, the department's top big-game specialist, was sent to Isle Royale for the winter, with Ellsworth St. Germain as helper, to undertake the first known experiment in trapping and holding moose. He made his headquarters at the Johnson place, and that family wintered there again.

When the ice broke up in the Lake Superior harbors in April, Hickie and St. Germain had 11 moose confined in a stout corral, more or less tamed. They could have trapped more, but had no way to hold them for shipment. The Conservation Department's new *Patrol No. 1*, an 80-footer skippered by Capt. Allers, was assigned the moving job. I was in the party that went to Isle Royale aboard the motorship.

Hickie had advised his superiors in Lansing by radio that he anticipated a hard job. The captive moose spooked easily, he warned, usually ran the wrong way, and were peevish.

"In your radio messages you have frequently said 'if,' 'but,' and 'hope to,'" he concluded. "Same here."

Those moose were the scruffiest-looking animals I had ever seen. Most of their long winter hair had been shed, but some still hung in ragged patches. Their necks and shoulders were festooned with repulsive purplish-gray moose ticks as big as small grapes, and the bulls were starting to grow short, clubby, unattractive antlers. They bore scant resemblance to the majestic animals I had photographed around the lakes in summer, and they proved as ornery as they were scruffy.

We worked them gingerly into the shipping crates by first baiting them into spacious live traps with a drop door at either end. The door the moose faced had a smaller door built in, the height and width of a shipping crate. The crate was set in place, the small door opened, and we prodded the moose into the crate with a moose plow, an ingenious contraption devised by Hickie and St. Germain.

The width of the livetrap and five feet high, it was built on skids, with a heavy plank floor that sloped up from the front end at a 45° angle. The back door of the trap was raised a few inches, the plow shoved under, and then while the door was slowly raised the plow was skidded ahead and the moose forced into the crate.

Some of them weighed 1,000 pounds or more, the crates at least 500, and we had no horses or power equipment. We put rollers under the crates and rolled them by hand. The job proved everything Hickie had predicted. The biggest bull evaded the baited traps for a day, but entered one in the night, and the project was completed. Shipped to Houghton, the moose were trucked to the Cusino Wildlife Area near Munising and released there.

The trapping operation was expanded the following winter, with a pulpwood camp on Siskiwit Bay as the base. Teams and manpower were available there, and Hickie wintered with a five-man crew. A total of 69 moose were trapped, but only 38 survived to reach the mainland. The project was continued a third winter, following a disastrous fire in the summer of 1936, and resulted in the capture of 25 more moose.

In all, 71 were released in three mainland areas, at Cusino, on the tip of the Keweenaw Peninsula, and in the Escanaba River Game Area. The entire stocking disappeared in a few years. A few were killed accidentally. State game men believed the rest succumbed to deer brain worms, a parasite that moose cannot tolerate. My own theory is that persistent poaching was the chief reason for the total failure of the stocking project.

As for the Isle Royale herd, it dropped to an estimated 150 animals and then began a slow comeback. Today timber wolves appear to be keeping moose numbers in balance with the food supply. Certainly there are far fewer moose now than in the 1920s.

The big island holds one other attraction that is fascinating and unique— its prehistoric copper pits. Copper occurs in the ancient lava flows, in the form of pure metal rather than ore, and Isle Royale was the scene of stone-age copper mining 2,000 to 3,000 years before the birth of Christ.

Early Americans crossed Lake Superior, presumably stayed through the summers, and worked the copper free from the rocks by clever, even if primitive, methods. They located outcrops of the metal, lighted fires over them, broke the heated rock with cold water. Then, using oval beach boulders as mauls and hammers, most of them without handles, they freed the sheets and chunks of copper.

They excavated thousands of pits, some 30 feet across and 15 to 20 feet deep. Countless broken and battered hammer stones were left in the pits, and crumbling ladders, charred wood, fire-blackened rock, fish scales, and other evidence of human work have been found in them.

In the last few centuries before white men reached Lake Superior, the miners were probably pottery-making Algonquin and Iroquois Indians. Broken pot sherds dug up in abundance at several camp sites on the Island (along with the bones of beaver, deer, moose, and caribou), revealed this. In all likelihood, the first miners, who began the work more than 40 centuries ago, were ancestors of these latecomers. But many questions about them remain unanswered.

Isle Royale became a national park in the 1930s. Many changes have come since. The Island is still roadless, but veined with hiking trails. It hosts more than 16,000 visitors a year, many of them hikers and backpackers.

But thimbleberry still grows beside the trails, loons still break the dawn stillness with their haunting cries, there is still good pike fishing in many of the lakes and moose feeding in their shallows. There are the copper pits on whose rim the hiker can stand and speculate about the dark-skinned miners who dug them with fire and beach boulders.

To me, Isle Royale is today what it was when I saw it first, a place of wilderness enchantment too profound to be explained.

The winter that began in December of 1930 was exceptionally mild, and at the end of January the ground was still bare of snow over most of southern Michigan. You may wonder how I happen to remember weather details of that kind 50 years back. I had good reason.

Shortly after daybreak on Feb. 2, I was due to lift off with two companions, in a single-engine Stinson aircraft, from the airport at Grand Rapids, where I was then living and working as outdoor editor of the *Grand Rapids Press* and seven other Booth Newspapers.

Our destination was Isle Royale, an isolated wilderness island in Lake Superior some 50 miles north of the Keweenaw Peninsula, one of Michigan's most beautiful scenic places and in winter one of the loneliest as well, locked in isolation and totally unpeopled.

Ours would be the first winter flight ever attempted to that remote, lake-girt, 50-mile-long finger of land that was the state's northernmost outpost. Because of the bare-ground conditions we would have to leave Grand Rapids with the Stinson wheel-equipped. We knew we could expect 18 to 36 inches of snow on Isle Royale. Landing on wheels in that much snow would be a tricky and risky feat of airmanship. But we carried heavy steel skis in the plane and were counting on a chance to exchange the wheels for the skis somewhere along the way. That hope proved vain, however.

The two men who would make the flight with me were Walter Hastings, staff photographer of the Michigan Conservation Department, and George Austgen, a Grand Rapids pilot with two or three years of winter flying experience in northern Michigan. Hastings was recognized at that time as one of the outstanding wildlife photographers in the country, and Austgen had made daily winter flights from Grand Rapids to Petoskey more times than he could remember. Both men were well qualified for what we were undertaking.

Ours was no daredevil stunt, undertaken for thrills or passing fame. The flight had been carefully organized by the papers for which I wrote as a major step in awakening public interest in Isle Royale and arousing support for a fledgling drive to protect and preserve its wilderness character by making it a national park.

Ben East with Stinson aircraft.

The campaign had been launched early in the 1920s by Albert Stoll, Jr., outdoor editor of the *Detroit News*. The drive was making slow headway, however, because very few Michigan residents, and almost nobody outside the state, had heard of Isle Royale, knew where or what it was, and in general the public could not have cared less what happened to it.

That was a time of aggressive conservation in Michigan, but people can hardly be expected to rally behind a protection campaign if they know nothing about what needs to be protected. The Booth editors shared my belief that a spectacular winter flight to the far-north island would do much to awaken public awareness of its existence and unique importance.

I had first visited the Island in the summer of 1926 and had fallen completely under the spell of its wild and rugged beauty. I had joined Stoll in his efforts to promote the national park project, but the goal seemed close to unattainable. I was convinced the winter flight would give it a substantial boost.

On top of that, the flight represented for me the realization of a dream. From the time I had first set foot on Isle Royale's rocky shores nearly five years before, I had been possessed by a wish to see the great island in its garb of winter loveliness.

I wanted to see the ridges and valleys when snow lay deep on them. I wanted to hike through the moss-bearded forests of spruce and balsam fir when their branches bent low with it. I wanted to watch wintry seas break at the foot of jutting headlands and fling streamers of spray high up the ice-hung walls. I wanted to savor the isolation and splendor of this island, decked in snow and ice, under the radiance of a winter moon and the eerier radiance of the Northern Lights.

Now I was to get my chance.

The most direct route from Grand Rapids to Isle Royale would have led us north to the Straits of Mackinac, over the Upper Peninsula to the Keweenaw Point, and then across Lake Superior to the Island. But that would have involved a 55-mile flight over Superior's ice fields and open water, and that was a risk we were not willing to take in a single-motor land plane. Instead we would go around the south end of Lake Michigan to Chicago, northwest to Duluth, and then up the north shore of Superior to a point opposite Isle Royale. That would leave only 14 miles over water and broken ice. The Island lies much nearer the Minnesota and Ontario shore than to Michigan.

We landed at Chicago to refuel and get maps of the country ahead. I still recall a flyer there warning us that the rest of our flight was over bad country. And at Wisconsin Rapids later in the day we were told that what awaited us was "just plain poison." Cross-country bush flying was still in its infancy then, and the warnings were not exaggerated.

To our disappointment, we landed at Duluth on an airport bare of snow. That meant we could not use our skis. We'd have no choice but to risk landing on wheels on Isle Royale, however deep the snow might be.

We left Duluth the next morning under a cloudless winter sky, and weather reports promised us ideal flying weather up the north shore of Lake Superior. But less than an hour on our way we learned that that giant lake makes its own weather, winter or summer, and it is weather that cannot be predicted.

Black clouds loomed ahead, and we flew into as savage a blizzard as I have ever seen. Snow in solid sheets blotted out everything in sight, gale winds tossed the aircraft like a chip, and the cloud ceiling dropped lower and lower. The north shore of Superior is no place for that kind of flying. Austgen drove the Stinson ahead for 30 minutes. His gloves were drenched with perspiration from gripping the wheel, and finally he banked around and headed back to Duluth.

We tried it again the following day, and, although we again ran into a lake-born snowstorm, it was a mild one and we pushed through until we could see the low dark line of Isle Royale in the gray-and-white expanse of Superior off our right wingtip. Austgen banked steeply and we were over the lake. For the next few minutes we asked only that the J-5 Wright Whirlwind motor keep up its steady roar.

Before we left Duluth I had talked on the phone with a Coast Guard officer at Two Harbors, Minnesota, who had taken a search party to Isle Royale by boat early in January to look for a missing trapper who had intended to winter on the Island with two companions. The officer told me that because of the mild winter none of the Isle Royale harbors was frozen sufficiently to permit a safe landing with our aircraft. Some of them still showed open water, he said.

I had also learned, by phoning Port Arthur, Ontario, that Thunder Bay was frozen solidly and that the inland lakes in that area were carrying 18 inches of ice, more than enough for us to land on. For us to set down on an inland lake on Isle Royale would mean some hard snowshoeing, packing our supplies and equipment down to the home of a summer fisherman where we would make our headquarters, but it was obvious we had no choice.

As we flew over Isle Royale at about 5,000 feet, we could see the great rugged Island spread out beneath us for its entire length of 50 miles, dotted with snow-covered lakes, shores indented with narrow bays and harbors, long parallel ridges of ancient lava giving it the appearance of a giant washboard.

No one, not even those who have cruised around Isle Royale by boat or those who have tramped its dim trails, crossed its ridges, and followed its valleys, can imagine its wild and haunting beauty as we saw it that day, mile high in the winter sky, its shores decked with ice, its cliffs and forests buried under a mantle of snow. It was worth all our long and hazardous flight to carry away that one mental picture of this wilderness place of majesty and beauty.

We circled the Island at an elevation of 1,000 feet or so, looking for a landing place and also hoping to spot moose from the air. We failed in the latter, but had no real difficulty in picking a lake to land on.

The previous summer I had spent two days with Holger Johnson, a commercial fisherman from Minnesota, at his summer home on Chippewa Harbor on the south shore of Isle Royale. He had given me permission to use his place, a snug log house of three rooms and a loft, with the sheltered harbor in front and timbered ridges behind, as our base if we made the winter flight.

The lake nearest the Johnson cabin, big enough for us to land on, was Richie, three miles inland. There was no trail, but a worn moose runway angled down to Chippewa Harbor, parallel to the small stream that was the lake's outlet. I had walked that trail several times in summer. It would serve our purpose.

A mile to the east of Richie and 500 feet above the ridges, Austgen turned into the wind and slanted down for his approach. This was the most critical minute of the entire trip. How deep was the blanket of snow on Richie? What would happen when we put our wheels down in it? We had no way of knowing, but we'd find out very shortly.

Then, to the amazement of Hastings and myself, the pilot poured coal to the motor and pitched toward the level white plain of the lake in a screaming power dive. At almost the last instant, when we flashed over the hills that frowned down on the lake, clearing the treetops by no more than 100 feet, we understood the reason. Winds sweeping the three-mile length of Richie swirled over those hills in broken turmoil, like water in a rapids. We tossed and plunged through that turbulence like a leaf in a gale. Had we come in at stalling speed a crash would have been inevitable.

Then we were over Richie, few yards above the ice, the Stinson losing speed and riding smoothly.

Halfway down Richie a good-sized island lifted out of the lake. Wise in the ways of winter flying, Austgen had picked his landing place close to the shore of that island, where winds might have swept most of the snow away.

BOREALIS

He set the wheels down on eight inches of wind-packed snow and we rolled to a stop as if we were on an airport runway. Fifty feet off our right wingtip snow was drifted along the brushy shore of the island to the height of a man's shoulders.

A long narrow arm of Lake Richie ran south toward Chippewa Harbor for almost a mile. We decided to taxi to the end of it and tie the Stinson down there, where it would be sheltered by timbered ridges on two sides, and also where our snowshoe trek to the Johnson place would be shortened by that mile.

We had taxied less than 100 feet when the wheels broke through thin ice and dropped to the hubs in slush and snow. The plane stopped as abruptly as if it had hit a solid wall.

The weight of almost two feet of snow on Lake Richie had settled the ice, allowing water to flood it and form a foot of thick slush. A crust of new ice an inch or so thick had formed on top, and a few inches of new snow had covered that, hiding the trap underneath. Had we set our wheels down in that slush the Stinson would have been demolished. George Austgen had chosen with superlative judgment his place to touch down. The formation of slush in that manner is a common occurrence on north-country lakes and rivers in periods of heavy snow, and the pilot had known what to expect. We had landed in the only safe area on Richie.

We could not leave the plane to freeze its wheels in the slush. Getting it back to hard ice proved a difficult chore. Austgen held the aircraft horizontal by gunning the motor to lift the tail off the ice, with the slush acting as brakes. Hastings and I endured the slip stream and pushed the tail around a foot or two at a time, until the Stinson was facing the small island. Then, using an ax and our snowshoes as shovels, we broke a short runway through the slush and shell ice for each wheel. Austgen pushed the motor to full throttle, Hastings and I shoved on the wing struts, and the plane moved slowly back to solid footing.

There we cut holes through 18 inches of hard ice, thrust poles in place underneath and tied down the wings and tail. The Stinson was safely anchored until we were ready to leave.

I doubt George Austgen ever forgot the snowshoe trek to the Johnson place late that afternoon. We packed as lightly as we could, taking only enough supplies for supper and breakfast, a few canned goods that would freeze if left in the plane, our sleeping bags, and belt axes. But Austgen had never used

Chippewa Harbor.

snowshoes before, and his harness fitted poorly. Before the hike was half finished he took the webs off and plodded through knee-deep snow without them. At least he could get his feet over logs without doing a falling leap or a tailspin, he told us. But when he finally pulled his boots off in the Johnson cabin his socks were wet with blood from the ill-fitting harness.

The last half mile he had to stop frequently for short rests. Hastings went ahead to get a fire going, and the pilot and I inched after him. Darkness had fallen by the time we stepped out of the timber into the clearing around the cabin, and I can remember no sight more welcome than the yellow square of lamplight framed by a kitchen window.

We stayed for 11 days, the only humans on Isle Royale. We did not carry a two-way radio, and no one knew whether we were safe on the Island, down somewhere in the wilderness country, or even at the bottom of Lake Superior. We had come expecting isolation, and we found it in full measure.

BOREALIS

Those 11 days are half a century behind me now, but a few of the things that happened I will remember as long as I live.

I recall a clear cold night, with the thermometer at 20 below, when the full moon climbed above Lake Superior outside the harbor entrance, laying a path of radiance across the restless water and lighting with almost noontime brightness the spruce-crowned ridges behind our cabin. There is a magic quality in winter moonlight on snow, and the magic is even more potent when the moonlight falls on ice-hung cliffs and dark unpeopled forests.

There was another night when the Northern Lights flung their ghostly banners across half the sky, faintly tinted with pink and green, in a silent display as beautiful as I have ever seen.

There were dawns when the colors in the east beggered description, and windless days when the brooding hush of the northern wilderness lay over everything, a silence that could be felt, when no branch stirred, no bird called, no living thing moved in the white, frozen world.

But there were wild neighbors around us, and most of the time they made their presence known. Coyotes yapped from the ridges at dawn and dusk, moose fed on the tops of the birches we cut for firewood and bedded only 100 yards from our door. We put out table scraps on an improvised tray, and Canada jays, the whiskey jacks of woodsmen, carried them away and cached them as fast as we replenished the supply.

One other bird reminded us of his presence time after time. He was a great horned owl that lived along the moose trail we followed from Lake Richie to Chippewa Harbor. We never saw him, but we knew he was there. He first sounded his deep, dismal hooting one evening when we came along the trail as dusk was deepening. We suspected he resented our intrusion into his world of winter solitude, and from then on we heard his dim, hollow cries whenever we passed that way, by day or in the half light of evening. He would begin to hoot long before we were near him and continue until we passed out of hearing. Once he left the fur of a snowshoe rabbit in the trail, as if he were serving notice of the kind of hunter he was.

In one of the major goals of the trip we failed completely. That was to see and photograph moose from the air. In all the flying we did before our landing and again after takeoff when we left, we did not spot one of the animals.

We found their tracks wherever we went, and we jumped them feeding in thickets or bedded in the snow on the ridges. We even cut balsam trees for bait, hoping to lure them in for pictures. But in the 11 days we caught no more than a few very brief glimpses of the big animals.

We had also wanted to learn as much as we could about their winter food supply and condition. It was plain that the entire Island was being over-browsed, but we saw nothing to indicate that starvation was imminent. I know now that that was because we did not know how to interpret the evidence. Three years later, at the end of winter in 1934, moose would be dying of hunger by the score in every part of Isle Royale.

One other good memory I have from that winter adventure. That is of the day I crossed the Island on snowshoes, a round trip of 22 miles, by myself. Hastings stayed at the camp in the hope of making moose pictures. I can still see my solitary line of tracks leading up the ridges and across the snow-covered lakes, still hear the eerie howling of a coyote who discovered my presence, although I saw nothing of him, and serenaded me all the while I hiked the ice of Chickenbone Lake.

Two days before we were ready to take off for the flight home we went back to the plane to replace the wheels with skis. That was the first time Austgen had returned to Lake Richie since we landed. The change to skis gave us no problems, and we finished the job in a couple of hours. Then we started the motor and Austgen took the Stinson up for a short trial flight. We were ready to leave.

A raging blizzard smothered Isle Royale in snow the next day, but the morning of Saturday, Feb. 14, dawned clear and bright.

Our work at Michigan's farthest north was finished. We had seen the big snow-blanketed island in all the moods of winter, in the still cold of moonlight nights, and swept by wind-driven snow that all but hid the timbered ridges, and we had come to feel a strong attachment for Holger Johnson's snug log house that had sheltered us those 11 days.

We had cut firewood earlier to replace what we had used. We put the place in order, made up our packs, nailed the door shut as we had found it, on the remote chance that if before spring a stranded person needed to open it with his bare hands he would have no difficulty. Then we began the final hike to Lake Richie.

We knew nothing of it at the time, but to Hastings went the credit for being the last man to set foot on Isle Royale before Congress passed and President Hoover signed a bill authorizing the creation of a national park there. Unfortunately, the bill provided no funds for the project, but at least it was a forward step.

Hastings won the honor when he climbed out of the Stinson, stood at a wingtip and held up a handkerchief to give Austgen the wind direction for takeoff.

Once in the air, with the washboard of Isle Royale 1,000 feet below, we found ourselves bucking a strong headwind. We did not have enough fuel for the flight to Duluth under those conditions, so the pilot turned north instead, toward Port Arthur, Ontario. He set the skis down on the snow-covered ice of Thunder Bay, and in minutes some 200 to 300 curious Canadians ringed the Stinson. Ours was the third outside aircraft that had ever landed there.

We were treated with the utmost courtesy by Port Arthur officials and Canadian customs officers, and early the next afternoon, delayed by American customs in Washington, we lifted off the ice and headed down the Superior shore to Duluth.

We now confronted the reverse of our earlier flight. Then we had flown to a wheel landing in deep snow. The Duluth airport was bare of any hint of snow, and we would land on skis. I recall vividly the feeling in my stomach at the sight of an ambulance and three fire trucks lined up in front of the hangar, ready for an emergency dash to a burning aircraft.

It didn't happen. Austgen put the skis on the bare ground, the undercarriage crumpled on one side, a wing tip dug into the frozen earth and disintegrated, and the Stinson came around in a tight ground loop. But the three of us were hardly shaken. One final time George Austgen had proven himself a bush pilot who knew his trade.

The aftermath of the flight was even more than we had hoped for. The pictures we brought back, especially the strikingly beautiful movie film taken by Hastings, and the stories I wrote took the public by storm. For the first time, the people of Michigan saw Isle Royale and began to understand its importance.

Hastings and I teamed up in an illustrated lecture about the flight, using his film, and drew turn-away audiences wherever we appeared. Our experience at Grand Rapids, when we launched the show, was typical. We opened in the largest auditorium then available, a church that seated 1,700, and turned away more than could be admitted. We repeated a week later, and the overflow was even larger. When 5,000 were unable to get into the church on a third try we gave up.

Public enthusiasm for the national park spread like wildfire. An Isle Royale National Park Association was organized, with a newspaperman friend of mine, Bill Duchaine of Escanaba, as the sparkplug. It attracted as members prominent conservationists from all over the country.

But until 1935 the park project remained at a standstill, for the reason that the federal government would not appropriate funds for the purchase of privately owned land on the island.

By that time U.S. Sen. Arthur Vandenberg of Grand Rapids had climbed aboard the bandwagon and was giving the park plan full support. In May of 1935 he carried an appeal directly to President Roosevelt, and in December of that year FDR, spurred by a major pulpwood cutting operation on the Island, set aside by executive order the needed $705,000 for "emergency conservation work" on Isle Royale. The road to land purchase was now open. The national park dream had become reality at last.

I have in my files today a bulging sheaf of the ups and downs the proponents had confronted, the hurdles they had cleared. Many people in and out of Michigan had worked long and hard in behalf of the project; many in high places and low had contributed to its success. It had taken 15 years from the time Albert Stoll first proposed it for it to attain the desired end.

Of all those who helped, I doubt that any made a more important contribution than our flight to the Island when it was locked in winter solitude, a place as isolated as could then be found anywhere in this country. That statement may have a boastful sound, but it certainly is not so meant.

The flight had been the adventure of a lifetime for my two companions and me. In addition, we took honest pride in bringing to the people of Michigan an understanding of the rugged loveliness of the state's northernmost land. And to have furthered the final happy outcome of the effort to preserve Isle Royale's wilderness was a source of deep satisfaction.

The Isle Royale Natural History Association thanks Michigan Out-of-Doors *Magazine and Ben East for permission to reprint this article which appeared in the January and February 1981 editions of the magazine.*

A Memorable Cruise

INTRODUCTION - *To escape the summer heat of Leavenworth, Kansas, Reverend Charles Parker Connolly and Judge Charles Dassler and their extended families made their annual pilgrimage to Isle Royale. After a number of years of camping, both families became devotees of Isle Royale and built summer homes perched on a cliff in Tobin Harbor. This narrative of discovery, understatement, parody, and humor chronicles the making of family bonds to the Island. For Reverend Connolly, discovery was a part of the spell of Isle Royale and he sought out its charms, having relocated old surveyors' trails to Mount Franklin and Lake Desor, and a new trail to Lookout Louise. The Island has changed remarkably since 1908. What for the "adventurers" was Fish Island, inhabited by Swedish and semi-American fishermen, became Belle Isle, with a relatively luxurious resort and, later, today's campground. "Double Island" became Booth and Grace islands; trails into the interior were virtually nonexistent. "The scene of the crime," Captain Francis' pound-net fishery based out of Birch Island, is gone, as are traces of "the grave" at Todd Harbor, located somewhere near the present-day group sites. The determined pursuit by the "cruisers" of brook trout is sometimes repeated today, but the distinctive "era" of brook trout fishing immediately before and after the turn of the century is gone too.*

Reverend Connolly died in 1960 at the age of 91. Fortunately, his tongue-in-cheek memoir of his week-long expedition allows a sense of discovery and humor to live on.

THE CREW AND THE START

Listen my children and you shall hear
Of Captain Carl and his dangers drear.

29

BOREALIS

In the year of our Lord 1908, on August the thirteenth, but one day before Friday (ye superstitious sign), a notable voyage of immortal discovery was begun by four dauntless mariners. This invincible quartet of reckless rovers, to the consternation of all the fishermen of Tobin Harbor, started in a sixteen-foot launch towing two row-boats to make a journey of over a hundred miles around Isle Royale, Michigan, in Lake Superior, Longitude 87, Latitude 48. The reckless four were Mr. Charles F. W. Dassler, a high-strung, nervous man and sound sleeper, Mr. Carl Dassler, the tirelessly taciturn, Mr. Wilder Lawrence, the incessantly loquacious, and Mr. Charles Parker Connolly, the phlegmatic.

The start was made at 2:25 P.M. Treacherous Blake Point was speedily passed in silence and then Dame Nature proceeded to baptize the devotees of Neptune. A thunder shower inspected the craft and crew with something more than a fall of dew, in fact a trifle more than they thought due. Fish Island was at last sighted and reached at 4:24 P.M. Thanks to the hospitality of Mr. Johnson, the mariners were not compelled to pitch tent in the damp. One of the cottages on "Paradise Avenue," as the sign board modestly announced, offered the luxury of shelter and stove. A semi-American meal was eaten on a Swedish table. Schafskopf kept the mariners on an intense intellectual strain until bed time, when Captain Carl, Mate Charles, and Steward Wilder slept on the floor. As the boards were undressed, they remained dressed, on the theory that opposites attract. The Chaplain was graciously permitted to share the bed of a Swedish fisherman employed by ye host Johnson. Suffice it to say that the Swede slept with the Chaplain, but the Chaplain did not sleep with the Swede.

McCARGOE COVE AND ITS PISCATORIAL PRODIGALITY

Listen my children and you shall shout
What mammoth pickerel, what bonny trout.

At 8:11 A.M. the entire crew and the whole squadron launched forth on the deep, bound for McCargoe Cove. Arriving there at 9:13 A.M., the flotilla was left in the charge of the sagacious Mate while the rest of the crew proceeded upon a piscatorial investigation. The printed reports of the varieties and species of fish to be found in these waters (the discerning reader is invited to carefully consider the foregoing phrase "to be found") may be read in the Government Special, Volume 13, pp. 13 to 13,000. They make special mention in that voluminous and creditable report of the fine brook trout grounds encountered, but seem to have no grounds for discussing the trout themselves. People who are surfeited themselves often forget how delightful trout are to others, and even a description of a great catch is more interesting than sheer silence. One must not be too exacting, however, of mere fishermen. These mariners were immortal sailors not illustrious authors.

At the head of the cove there is a stream, and in that stream there was something. The whole three-fourths of the crew sustained a most unexpected shock when a small lake trout, or a large brook trout, or something else, suddenly, without any preliminary announcement, took hold of the trolling spoon and as suddenly spat the spoon out. The scenery proved somewhat more numerous than the piscatorial specimens mounted. The Captain with his eagle-eye sighted a bunch of birches and his camera soon did its deadly work.

The old wharf of the copper plant was discovered by the mariners, cat tails were gathered, and more pickerel grounds were cited. "We did not get our pick of the pickerel," observed one sad fisherman of the party.

This second chapter of the cruise of the cliff dwellers must end with the praiseworthy chronicle that up to this time there had been no complaint, much less sign of mutiny on the part of the sailors, because of the steady diet of fresh fish.

Todd's Harbor, Brook Trout, Hatchet Lake, and Sundry Invisibilities Seen by the Crew

Listen my children and you shall Grin
At the Tale of Tail and Scales and Fin.

McCargoe Cove was left at 1 p.m. by Mate Dassler's chronometer. The voyage to Todd's Harbor was smooth and without incident.

The boats were beached high, tents were pitched, and the crew started forth with special strings under coats to preserve the huge catch of brook trout in the famous creek to the west of their camp. The stream was reached, the lines were feverishly dropped, and great quantities of brook trout were taken from the stream—by others last Fourth of July. The Mate, having some legal

BOREALIS

lore, bethought himself of a new method (though not unfamiliar to some
courts of law) of catching fish and succeeded in obtaining a white fish, where-
upon in a lucid interval, the Chaplain asked no questions but ate fish. For
further particulars one must consult the pound net of Captain Francis of
McCargoe Cove.

The next day, Sunday morning, Captain Francis lifted the net and the
whole crew enjoyed the spectacle of squirming fish. No matter how many fish
one catches, they always enjoy seeing others, so that their delight in this
spectacle must not be attributed to any eccentricity on the part of the cruisers.

The day previous (i.e., Saturday) the crew started to discover the trail to
Hatchet Lake. Variously bedoped they plunged into the wilderness. Certain
marks on certain trees provoked considerable discussion. Whether they were
knots or not, whether they were blazes or not, divided the crew into rival and
contentious parties, for we all devoutly wished to go by blazes. It seemed at last
to be unanimously decided that the trail was not discovered and surmounted.
But the weary travellers were well repaid for their tireless perseverance, for at
last the glorious vision of Hatchet Lake burst upon their vision.

Hatchet Lake is shaped like George Washington—it cannot lie, for the
party did not once discover a place where it lies. It is full of brook trout,
according to the Chaplain. It is dried up, according to the Captain. It is
surrounded by a swamp, according to the Mate. The Steward has thus far
expressed no idea concerning the Lake. Two features of this memorable inland
trip will never be forgotten. The large, luscious, and abundant blueberries and
raspberries which refreshed the weary sailors, and the smooth, elastic rocks
upon the high cliffs. These rocks were found in several piles surrounded by
broken bits of copper-bearing rocks. It is surmised that the Indians used them
in mining copper. Some of the old trenches (Costeans) made by the copper
mining companies were also discovered and a few large mosquitoes and other
treasures. Weary, but still undaunted, the crew returned to camp after a seven
hours' battle with rocks, swamps, fallen trees, tangles, bushes, and insects.
They report that the inland lake fishing is good—for others.

Sunday afternoon, a grave on the hill was visited, a snake killed, an old
journal discovered full of entries concerning supplies used by an old mining
company once located there, and a supper prepared to be eaten en route. The
sailors started Sunday evening to let the gasoline do the work, and Captain
Carl the steering, for the ever hopeful mariners. The precise time of departure
was 6:30 P.M.

32

LITTLE TODD AND A BIG FISH

Listen our Ladies, and you shall know
How they rode the Waves and broke the Tow.

O n Sabbath evening, just at sunset, the merry mariners resumed their voyage.

In the Harbor the waves were low, but out on the open Lake they proved higher, and kept rising as the wind rose. The little launch behaved perfectly, never missing an explosion and leaping up on the waves with an easy confidence. The sailors ate as they sailed with the spray flying in their faces, but not all the spray could wash away their pleasant smiles. The rear row-boat, being a very virtuous craft, imagined that the launch was too fast a companion, so it broke away from its leader and went drifting about. Captain Carl thereupon skillfully mended the tow line amid the bouncing waves, while the crew looked on in admiration. As the wind and waves kept getting higher it was unanimously decided to put into Little Todd's Harbor. There the tents were pitched just as the darkness settled about the sailors. A thunder shower was specially gotten up for the party and proved an entire success, blowing over the Captain and Mate's tent so that they were compelled to dress again (the process consisting in the assumption of a necktie and morning smile on Carl's part and a shirt or so by the Mate), and the guys then repaired and tightened the guy lines.

The next morning it blew for a change and the mariners cooked their breakfast on the fisherman's stove. The Captain described the Mate's efforts to sleep with the small of his back on the top of a rock and his head at the foot of the hill on one side and his feet at the bottom of the hill on the other side. The Mate prefers sleeping on the ground to any of the modern newfangled luxuries, but he was strangely reticent about the delights of his slumber the first night at Little Todd's. Meanwhile, the Captain, with a determined gleam in his serene eyes, announced his ultimatum. "I shall make a bed."

After breakfast the Captain and the Chaplain started for brook trout. They groped, crawled, wormed, sneaked, sprawled, and otherwise betook themselves through two miles of impediments too numerous and profane to describe. At last the trout stream was discovered. The Captain has a rise immediately. The Captain had a second rise. The Captain had no more signs and stretched himself out to sleep. The Chaplain was determined to discover the nature of the elusive thing that the Captain failed to land. He tried various flies and at last landed a huge brook trout, being at least four inches long all at one time and in one place. With this coveted and invaluable prey the party returned, but found that the heavy weight of the fish added much to the discomfort of their return. They arrived in time for dinner, after which raspberries were plucked fresh from the bushes, the white caps were watched, the wind was felt, the sky was scrutinized, and the Captain went into the furniture business. At sunset the party climbed a fine cliff to the north of the fisherman's settlement, while the Captain in a playful fit of deceitfulness took a moonlight view of the setting sun. That night some of the sailors again slept since it seemed the only thing left to do.

Early in the morning (3:40 A.M.) the Chaplain called all hands to rise. The wind had partially subsided, the waves were lower. After breakfast one of the fishermen with a quiet air of Finnish finality announced that "Him will clear up." Another fisherman, surveying the same lake, clouds, sky, etc., calmly announced, "Him will blow." The mariners decided that "Him will clear up" was the proper prognostication and they sailed forth. "Him" blew a little worse. The Mate by a miscalculation misled the Captain as to his whereabouts.

Meanwhile, "Him" was blowing some more. Now for the first time the situation looked a trifle ominous. The shore was rocky with no immediate prospect of a favorable place for landing. The waves kept getting higher. Fortunately, the sailors had purchased a new tow line at Little Todd's some eighty feet long, so that they had no fear of another broken line. The spray kept spraying and "Him" kept blowing. At last a fisherman's boat was spied. As the launch neared it, the skippers saw that the fishermen had poured oil on the troubled waters, which so mollified them as to make it easy for the launch to turn broadside and enter a cove, which, to the delight of the mariners, the fishermen announced as "Huginnin Cove."

After a council of war it was agreed that the Captain and Mate should go on to Washington Harbor, six miles away, mail cards, and return with butter for the crew. The little launch bobbed up and down, riding the waves gracefully and without danger. Meanwhile, the Steward and Chaplain discovered another trout stream but did not fish the stream, not only because of the weariness of catching fish perpetually, but chiefly because the stream had no water in it. The sailors had learned before this that a dried-up stream is not quite so likely to contain an abundant supply of fish. Still they do not wish to be confident concerning the habits of brook trout, their only dogmatic and insistent affirmation being that they know nothing about brook trout and believe that no one else does. They then returned, having found a pen knife by the trout stream, made a camp fire, pitched the tents and hungrily awaited the return of their partners.

They came with faces full of spray rainbowed with smiles as they told of the brave little craft's plucky encounter with the waves, of their timely arrival, of the steamer *Easton's* appearance, and of their deep abysmal appetite. The crew ate no fish at that meal so that they would not become surfeited with the bounty of the Lake. The Chaplain regretted his inability to kill a wild duck near the cliff. The stones thrown by the Steward and himself had caused the duck to depart from the scene, but not from the flesh.

The waves having gone down in the night, the mariners voted to leave *terra firma* and seek Neptune's domains again.

WASHINGTON HARBOR, THE BROOK TROUT, THE CARIBOU, AND OTHER DISCOVERIES

Listen sweet ladies and you shall know
That the Washington Harborites saw a great show.

We left the Cove at 11:22 A.M. and arrived at Washington Harbor just as the steamer from Port Arthur arrived with an excursion party.

Washington Harbor is a summer resort for people who have more clothes than they can display at home and who need a quiet place where they can act as a peg upon which to hang their fashionable gowns. The men wear golf clothes, chiefly because of the absence of golf. The women wear white skirts and other absurdities. The mariners mused upon these visions as they walked down the board walk. That walk down the board walk has become one of the deathless traditions of the famous resort. At last, four happy-looking mortals, properly clothed, properly dirty, had appeared as happy ghosts at their unhappy banquet. The languid ladies bristled with interest and followed the blissful mariners with their envious eyes. Here were men living the simple life and daring to be happy. "How preposterous," sighed Dame Fashion. Undismayed by feminine eyes and sexless cameras focused upon them, the sailors reeled on. A board walk beneath their feet felt as uncertain as a merry-go-round. They continued to lift their feet high in the air to avoid rocks that were not there.

BOREALIS

Still the ladies stared. Still the sailors lumbered down the board walk. At last, after re-stocking with provisions and gasoline, the crew started down the Harbor.

The Captain and Chaplain found some more most promising grounds which they fished with a pathetic patience. Being so near civilization, they determined it would be prudent not to catch more than the law permits. They discovered the Club House, the seat of the old copper mine, and actually beheld with their own eyes upon Isle Royale a horse, a cow, and a pig. This vision filled them with such amazement that they returned to the camp in a pleasant little nook on the south shore of the Harbor, perhaps two miles from Singerville.

The phenomena of special significance and prominence must now detain the historian. First, the Mate forgot that he was a human being and, having found a particularly hard rock on which to comfortably lie, fell asleep and imagined himself a living fog horn. His lusty fog horn solo not only terrified the Chaplain who mistook it for a man-eating lion in the brush, but actually attracted some large animal which crashed through the underbrush and finally dashed off. It was afterward learned that the animal was probably a caribou.

Early the next morning the prospects in the Harbor seemed to warrant the continuance of the cruise, especially since it was more generous to leave the remaining brook trout for the people of the region. Accordingly the crew started, went to the mouth of the Harbor, discovered a storm raging, and returned to Double Island, where the boats were beached, and the sailors washed their faces, hands, and handkerchiefs and stretched out on the sand for a sun-bath. After this refreshing performance, which the Captain confided to his observing camera, the party made a fashionable call at Singerville, walking down the board walk again with such high-stepping as had not been witnessed there from time immemorial. The high cliff was surmounted, the view was taken by the sailors, and they returned to the exciting board walk again. It was still there in all its strange levelness. The dudes and dudesses tried to interpret the mysterious animals which thus had invaded their listless quarters, but the phenomenon was beyond comprehension.

The sailors found the fishermen more intelligent and communicative than the Singervilleites, so the Chaplain proceeded to accumulate information as to the weather. He explained to the first Finn that he found there was some discrepancy in the prognostications of sundry fishermen and asked him what might be relied upon as a sure thing. The Finn thereupon assumed an impres-

36

sive air of profound intelligence and gravely announced, "If him blows two days from the sou'west and you see clouds gathering in the nor'west, the wind will change."

The Chaplain rejoiced in the possession of one infallible deliverance and went to the second Finn expecting an unqualified corroboration. But the second Finn, when catechized as to the reliability of the sou'west, nor'west combination shook his head and drawled, "Sometimes."

"What, then, do you think is a sure thing?" queried the Chaplain.

"Well, I'll tell you," he said with an engaging air of confidence, "if he blows from the sou'west and you see clouds coming from the nor'east, him will blow like the devil."

Thereupon, the Chaplain made up his mind as touching one point. The fishermen are most happy in the first statement they invariably make, "Well, I don't know."

The next morning it was decided that it would be more prudent, since the weather was so uncertain, for the Steward and the Chaplain to take their row-boat and go home on the steamer *Easton*.

Heavily ballasted with a good meal and two pieces of apple pie, the Chaplain and Steward started forth, arriving in Tobin Harbor at six o'clock that evening to the infinite surprise of Rheinhardt, who thought that they had all died several deaths by that time.

This ends the tale so far as the semi-circumnavigators are concerned. The next chapters will relate the adventures of the circumnavigators, the Captain and Mate.

THE MATE'S ADDENDUM

THE PARTING OF THE WAYS—THE START IN THE WAVES—THE CRUISE ON THE WAVES—THE ARRIVAL AT FISHERMAN'S HOME

The Chaplain and the Steward left Double Island Camp about 9:30 A.M. on Friday, August 21, in the Chaplain's row-boat, taking with them their belongings. The food supply was left for the subsistence of the Captain and the Mate, as it seemed uncertain when the remaining half of the crew would reach the home port. The crew thus parted in twain. The Captain and the Mate, after a re-arrangement of the camp, at about 11 A.M. (the scheduled time for the arrival of the good steamer *Easton*), rowed to the dock at Washington Harbor, where the Chaplain and the Steward were found anxiously searching the northerly entrances to the Harbor for some sign of the coming of the steamer.

The sou'wester that for almost five days had been continuously breaking on the rocky shores of the westerly ends of Isle Royale at this time gave no sign of abatement. About an hour later, the horizon in the north-west disclosed rapidly advancing clouds. In a very short time, these clouds, with a considerable breeze from the same quarter and a sprinkle of rain, suggested the advisability of seeking shelter, and the necessity of the Captain and Mate returning to Double Island to look after their camp, boats, and provisions. Good-byes were hurriedly spoken, and the Chaplain and Steward were left on the dock to await the arrival of the belated steamer.

Upon reaching camp all was secured against the threatening rainstorm. During the mid-day meal, the whistle of the *Easton* was heard, advising the crew of two that the semi-circumnavigators would soon be on their way to Tobin Harbor. The regular scheduled route of the steamer being along the south shores of Isle Royale, the Captain and the Mate scrambled through the forest on Double Island to an elevation near the south entrance to Washington Harbor to get a glimpse of their departing comrades when the *Easton* would pass through the narrow channel connecting Washington Harbor with Grace Harbor on the south. The departing signal of the steamer was heard, but no steamer passed through the channel. The crew of two concluded that the Captain of the *Easton* had abandoned the scheduled route, and headed his boat for the north shores of the Island to avoid the south-west rollers, this course promising a smoother voyage for his passengers. This we later learned was the fact, being told that there was quite a number of sea-sick passengers aboard, the steamer having experienced heavy seas before reaching Washington Harbor.

Again returning to the Camp, it was decided to make preparations for an early departure for the south shores of Isle Royale, to leave all unnecessary cargo, lighten the launch by transferring much that it had carried to the tow, and that thus it was possible, since the nor'wester was still breaking the crests of the sou'west rollers, for the boats and crew to at least reach Long Point, nine miles away. Everything having been made snug in the launch and in the tow, with provisions, boxes, and other not needed articles discarded, the tow was shoved out into the bay where it was picked up by the crew and securely fastened to the launch with 40 feet of tow line.

The start was made at 4:01 P.M. on Friday, August 21. In a few moments the sailors were riding the sou'west rollers. The course taken in passing through Grace Harbor was nearly directly S.W. The mariners were too much occupied in looking ahead, watching the tow, and getting into their slickers to admire the grandeur of the dashing of the waters against the steep cliffs and short gravel beaches on the shores of this Harbor. The newly built Government Lighthouse on the Rock of Ages, three miles out from the Harbor, was sighted and soon left behind.

Passing well outside the reefs extending into the Lake at the South Point (Cumberland Point) of Grace Harbor that were well marked by the seething mass of foam from the swells breaking over them, we rounded the South Point of Grace Harbor about 2 miles off shore. From this point we ran partly in and partly across the trough of the sea made by the incoming rollers from the sou'west that were somewhat broken at the crests by the nor'wester blowing across them. When in these rollers, the towering shores of the Island two to four hundred feet in height were sometimes not visible from the launch. The length of the waves may be approximated from the fact that the launch, tow line, and row-boat, 72 feet in length in passing across the swells, was often between the wavecrests. The beaches of the next southerly bay, known as Rainbow Cove, were almost hidden by the surf of the breaking waves.

The mariners debated some as to putting in at Long Point about nine miles from the starting point, but when opposite this point, as it would require careful and tedious steering to make the landing nearly two miles distant, it was decided to continue on the course for some more available landing farther up the coast and endeavor to make "Fisherman's Home" about eleven miles further on.

The boats were riding easier now, the highlands of the Island to some extent sheltering the navigators from the nor'wester, and the sou'west rollers bowling them merrily along. They ran thus for another hour, when the surface of the water gave indications of a wind coming from a different direction.

Presently, a threatening mass of dark, fast-moving clouds appeared from over the heights of the Island shore, apprising the sailors that a storm from the nor'east was about to cross their course. This nor'easter with a beating rain for an hour kept the navigators and everything in the launch well moistened, creating also as against the sou'west rollers a choppy sea.

When this unexpected local storm had spent its force, the sailors were nearing the vicinity of "Fisherman's Home," situated upon a spit of land and rock extending into the Lake parallel to the main shore of the Island, not far from the westerly entrance to Siskiwit Bay.

The ledges of rocks, islets, reefs, and shoals extending easterly into the Lake from opposite Point Houghton, some seven miles in extent, separating Siskiwit Bay from the Lake, were seen in the distance. Menagerie Island is one of this group, being the site of Isle Royale Light, also called Menagerie Island Light.

The crew of two, after debating whether to proceed on the voyage for the home port steering across the waters during the coming night by the Menagerie Island Light, concluded to put in at "Fisherman's Home," get warmed up, fill the fuel tank, and make the decision when there.

Darkness had settled on the waters intensified by the cloudy sky. It was quite a run to avoid shoals and rocks in order to reach the little harbor lying back of the spit. The inlet between the spit and the mainland was found to be narrow, the darkness rendering it impossible to determine the depth of water ahead. Just as the fishing village came in view, running slow, the keel of the boat touched the gravel bottom. Lights on shore (the villagers having heard the approach of the launch) directed us to the landing. A supper in a warm room and the offer of the storeroom floor for a bed soon settled the question about going farther on. The landing was made at 7:30 P.M.

When the sailors gave an account of themselves and informed the interrogators that the little boats had come from Washington Harbor since four o'clock that afternoon, the Norwegian fishermen appeared incredulous, saying that they did not see how we did it, as they had been caught out in their fishing boats during that afternoon's storm. The row boat seemed to take their eye, they examined it, and expressed admiration for its construction and lines. That the little launch should be able to make the run with its tow, without any mishap in the sea the boats had passed through, was a subject of comment.

Our host, Mr. Idius Seglem, on learning that we were from Scoville Point and that we knew Rheinhardt, became an old friend.

HOMEWARD BOUND—SISKIWIT BAY—THE FOREST FIRE— THE IMPATIENT TOW—THE HOME PORT

The Captain, no doubt having in mind a possible surprise of a string of brook trout for the Chaplain, suggested a run to Wright Island, lying nearly opposite to the starting point of the trail leading to Siskiwit Lake on the mainland.

Inquiring of the Finns, it was learned that a party from Duluth had been there the preceding week and caught brook trout by the hundreds. Since they left a forest fire had been raging for two days near the trail to the Lake.

It was surmised that this fire resulted from carelessness on the part of the members of this party in failing to properly guard and extinguish their campfires.

The voyagers got under way at 6:35 A.M. on Saturday, August 22. The quiet waters in the little haven were soon left behind. The navigators entered the strait to Siskiwit Bay at Point Houghton where the dense mass of smoke back of Wright Island seven miles away became visible. This suggested the advisability of abandoning the project of the Captain for a piscatorial investigation. The bow of the launch was thereupon headed for the indistinctly visible south shore of Isle Royale beyond the easterly entrance to Siskiwit Bay. "Him" commenced to blow. "Him" increased the blow. "Him" blowed more and more from the sou'west. When about opposite Menagerie Island Light, the tow became impatient at the slow progress of the launch and, under the impact of the variable westerly breezes, attempted to overtake its leader, necessitating the lengthening of the tow line from 40 feet to 80 feet, which extension was speedily effected.

Nearing Chippewa Harbor, a large gasoline boat, which proved to be the *City of Two Harbors*, was discovered hugging the shore, westward bound, about one and one-half miles on our port side. She seemed to be laboring in the adverse wind.

After passing the entrance to Chippewa Harbor well out, and when about opposite Lea Cove, the sailors decided to no longer keep the usual course along the shore to the old Rock Harbor Light, but to steer across the open Lake to Smithwick Channel. This course was then taken through a choppy sea, with an abundance of spray over our port side.

Entering Rock Harbor, through Smithwick Channel, it took but a short time to reach Scoville Point, rounding which we tied up at our home port, the little dock back of the cliff in Tobin Harbor, at 11:45 on Saturday, August 22, 1908.

Thus the cruise of the circumnavigators ended.

A Letter on Logging

INTRODUCTION - *Forty-two years after leaving the Island logging camp, James T. Wynne returned to the back-country to view again the site of Mead's logging operation in Siskiwit "swamp." Little remained of the camp, yet Jim was pleased to be back in the familiar location. Encamped at Siskiwit Bay Campground (superimposed on the former camp clearing and pulpwood stacks), Jim fondly recounted what life was like as an Island logger. These warm conversations stimulated Jim to write the following letter in 1978 describing camp life.*

The third logging operation on the Island, Mead's was by far the most significant. Jim Wynne's fellow "jacks" were agents of great environmental change, yet they were hardly in control of their own lives. Only its extreme isolation distinguishes the camp Wynne remembers from others scattered elsewhere in Minnesota and Michigan. Transient lumberjacks ate in silence in all camps and maintained a distinct code of conduct, which reveled in both chivalrous and bacchanalian behavior. Wynne captures the color of the camp with stories of moose attacking bulldozers, off-loading horses and gas drums into the lake, and the heady smell of 200 wet socks drying in the rafters at night.

Interesting in itself, the pulpwood operation also played a seminal role in the establishment of the Isle Royale National Park. Both the threat and the deed of "logging off the Island" spurred efforts to establish the park. And out of the remaining slash piles of tree limbs came the cataclysmic environmental event of this century, the 1936 forest fire. One-fifth of the Island burned taxing the meager capabilities of federal administrators to protect Isle Royale. Barely gone from the Island during the fire, the "jacks" and "jippos" never looked back. Jim Wynne's letter allows us to look back and appreciate these men who loved and logged the "north woods."

On July 17, my wife and I and our grandson, and Dennis Wynne, his wife, and three sons arrived at Windigo on Isle Royale. After we had signed

43

in, we left for a backpacking trip to Siskiwit Bay. On the trail we met Tim, a ranger (I didn't get his last name), and I told him I had worked in a logging camp there in the winter of 1935–1936. He seemed very interested and the next evening he and the ranger at Malone Bay came to see us at our shelter at Siskiwit. They wanted to know if I could give them any information about the logging camp or a description of the camp and what happened there that winter of 1935–1936. We greatly appreciated their kindness in arranging a ride for us to Malone Bay with a fisherman and his wife, and also radioing the *Voyageur* so that we could catch a ride back to Grand Portage.

In early May of 1935, my Uncle Everett Wynne, who was to be the fore-man for the operation, and John Lindbloom, a company supervisor, made the trip up to Siskiwit Bay to scout the area for the George Mead Paper Company of Michigan. On their initial trip, they looked for a place to build the camp, surveyed the timber to be cut, and, most importantly, laid out the logging roads. They had to be as level as possible.

In a few days they were back in Grand Marais [Minnesota] making plans for the big job ahead. Men had to be hired, and building materials had to be purchased—nails, windows, tarpaper, and some lumber. The first job back on the Island was to build a makeshift kitchen in which to cook the meals. Men began clearing trees and underbrush off the campsite and some started cutting timber for the buildings. Soon the camp began to take shape.

Sometime earlier a little beetle had killed much of the balsam and high-land spruce on the Island so there was plenty of dry wood to work with. In the buildings the only lumber used was for the doors. The rest of the construction was of logs and poles cut in the swamp. For the roofs, dry balsam poles were laid up and down from ridge to eave. Then this was covered with tarpaper and more poles were put on top to keep the wind from blowing the tarpaper off.

Soon more men arrived and the logging began. First the main logging road had to be cleared. All of the wood cut from the right-of-way was piled on either side. Some men laid out strips and "jippos" (piece cutters) began cutting. It was too far to walk morning and night, so out at the western edge of the timber jippos began building shacks to live in for the long winter. There were seventeen shacks in all, and these shacks ranged from three to six miles from the main camp.

This operation was quite a challenge to the men in charge. Not that it was larger than previous camps they had run, but there were so many things involved. So much equipment was needed for the logging operation, as well as food, clothing for the men, hay and feed for the horses, and gas and oil for the tractors. Once the shipping season was over and winter had set in, the men would be isolated from the rest of the world except by short wave radio.

Everett Wynne had been a woodsman all his life, having run camps for various companies back in Minnesota and working as a timber cruiser and a regular lumberjack. It was quite a feather in his hat to be chosen for this operation. He had the pick of the men he wanted to help him, and he chose wisely. Guy Angell was his straw boss—an old friend who was a good woodsman and an amiable fellow. He would be second in command—a foreman under a foreman—because one man couldn't be in all places at the same time. Ernest Sederberg was the clerk. His job was to run the company store, keeping track of the men's wages and their purchases at the wanigan as well as many other details. Then there was the cook and his crew. Everett knew he had to have a good one because the men demanded it. None of them wanted to be stuck on the Island all winter with a "heartburn specialist." His choice was a man named Sigurd Benson. The head cook ran the kitchen and baked all the pastries, bread, cake, pies, cookies, and doughnuts. The second cook was in charge of cooking the meat and vegetables (all under the watchful eye of Sigurd Benson). The cooks washed the dishes, peeled potatoes, set the tables, and waited on the men. There was no fooling around at mealtime and no talking. The men went in to eat as quickly and quietly as possible and then on outside again. They always sat in the same place at the same time.

Then there was the blacksmith and his helper. These lumber camp specialists could do anything with a piece of iron—even making logging chains. Usually the company would dump a pile of flat iron, angle iron, and various-sized rods out in back of the shop and the blacksmith made what was needed. His helper, or handyman as he was called, did all the work requiring wood—skidding drays and repair on the big sleighs. Maybe one of the blacksmith's most important jobs was shoeing the horses. Usually these shoes came as blanks and had to be fitted to each individual horse, big or small. Most horses were easy to shoe; but I've seen some that were really man-eaters and this took special equipment. A block and tackle was hung from the ceiling of the shop. Then the horse was pulled up off the floor in a sling to fight and squeal until he was played out. Then the shoes were applied.

Another important job was the barn boss whose job was to see that all the horses were cared for. He cleaned the barn, fed hay and oats, and saw to it that the teamsters curried and brushed their horses every evening. He also had to wake up early to have the kerosene lanterns lit and hanging in place, and the chimneys or globes had better be clean!

Next came the bull cook—maybe the most important man in camp. He carried all the water needed and cut and carried the wood for the bunk houses and cook shack. At nine o'clock at night he blew out the lamps and lit them again in the wee hours of the morning. In the morning the men were awakened by one of the kitchen crew blowing the camp horn. The same one used to call the men to eat at mealtime.

Late in the summer of 1935, a crew of C.C.C. [Civilian Conservation Corps—a Depression work program for unemployed] boys from Michigan arrived with their supervisor, Mr. Ellsworth St. Germain, and his wife. Their job was to trap live moose to be shipped back to the mainland the following spring. They immediately began building quarters to live in, and erected a good-sized corral as well as a number of traps in which to catch the moose. I don't remember how many moose were caught, but at one time there were quite a few. Many of them became sick and died from eating green alfalfa hay. It was too rich for their stomachs after being used to balsam browse.

About this time a doctor and his wife arrived to take care of the men in case of illness. They were Dr. Anthony Curreri and his wife, who was a nurse. So, in addition to Mrs. Wynne, there were two other women and a baby in camp. Occasionally, two fishermen and their wives would come for a short visit. They were Mr. and Mrs. Sam Johnson from Wright Island, and Mr. and Mrs. Sivert Anderson, who lived at Hay Bay Point.

By fall the landing where the pulp was to be piled (where the two shelters now stand) had been cleared and the jippos were cutting. The men had built a dock out into the lake a short distance west of where the Park Service dock is today.

Long before the freezeup and bad weather set in, all the materials and equipment, including horses and tractors, had arrived. Everything came by barge from Grand Marais, Minnesota. It was towed by a small tugboat, the *Elmar the 2nd*.

There were many loads—sixty or seventy head of horses and their harnesses and hay and oats to feed them all winter, and caterpillar tractors and hundreds of barrels of gas and oil. Also, there must have been twenty-five or thirty sleighs for the long hauls from the western edge of the cutting. Next came smaller items such as clothing and other necessities for the crew, iron for the blacksmith, saws, axes, and other tools. And last but not least, enough

Slash from the pulpwood operations.

meat, vegetables, and groceries to keep nearly two hundred hungry men contented all winter.

Most of the pulp was cut by the piece—it was four cents a stick, I think. Some places where the timber was scattered, men cut for monthly wages. The big handicap for the men was the deep snow. The lumberjacks cut and carried the pulp sticks out on their back to a trail which they cut down the center of their strip. Every pile had to have a small stick of pulp standing up and down at one end. This was the only way they could find the piles by spring as there was eight feet of snow by then. However, the weather was usually mild and I don't believe it got down to zero all winter.

After the cutting was completed, the skidding began. First, small tractors packed the snow in the skidding trails. Then the skidders loaded five cords onto each sleigh and hauled them out to the main logging road. There the sleigh pole was taken off and the sleds hooked together with cross chains. As many as twelve and fifteen sleighs were pulled to the landing at one time by one of the bigger tractors. The skidders were also paid by the cord so the company knew just about how much it cost to get the wood to the landing.

Barns had to be built for the horses out in the shacker areas. In most cases, the men that did the cutting also did the skidding. We were a sorry-looking crew each night when we were skidding—wet from head to foot. In spite of the damp, wet conditions, however, not one man had a cold all winter—not even a sniffle! About the time we were finished skidding (which was sometime the latter part of March), a man from Shack Nine was attacked by an owl and lost one eye. I lived in Shack Seven a short distance away and I remember the incident very well. Some of the men fashioned a stretcher out of poles and blankets and carried him to Siskiwit Bay. There a plane came from Port Arthur and took him to Duluth. Later in the summer he returned to camp, when the pulp was put in the lake.

In camps like this, no money ever changed hands. We men in the shacks bought all our groceries from the camp. The grocery bill was charged against our wages and divided by the number of men in each shack. Each man cooked a week at a time and the rest would wash dishes, cut and carry wood, and haul water. Other purchases of clothing, tobacco, etc., were charged against each man's account.

After a cutter had completed a strip, the company supervisor, John Lindbloom, came out and counted the sticks of pulp. This count, multiplied by four cents, was then credited to the cutter's account at the office. If the timber was good, fairly thick, and not too big, a man could cut from one hundred to one hundred fifty sticks a day. But there were many days when we cut far fewer. There were no chain saws then. We used what was called a one-man saw and it was about four-and-a-half feet long. When our saw became dull, we had to take it back to camp and exchange it for a sharp one. John Johnson was the saw filer, and a good one too, who had been with Everett Wynne for many years in various camps.

I had worked in other camps but this one was somewhat different. First, we had a bathhouse (sauna), which was not allowed in camps on the mainland. And there wasn't the usual lice and bedbugs.

Now, I'd like to leave the shack area and describe life and working condition at the main camp. The horn usually blew at five o'clock in the morning; and after we dressed and washed up we had a big breakfast—pancakes, fried potatoes, oatmeal, prune or raisin sauce, bacon and cake, cookies, and doughnuts, plus bread and oleomargarine. The "ole" was never colored in camps and looked like lard. Milk was canned evaporated and mixed with water about three to one. After breakfast we went back to the bunkhouse and waited for

Everett to kick the door open (no knob on it) and yell "All aboard!" In the evenings after supper the men in charge would meet at the office to plan the next day's work. If there were any changes in plan, Everett would pick the men out as they came out of the bunkhouse following the "All aboard!" It would still be dark as we walked to our work—as much as three miles. By that time it would be almost light enough to go to work. In the evening we worked until we couldn't see any more and then it was time to walk back to camp. The evening meals were the biggest and the men the hungriest. Pie was always served at dinner and supper and a man could eat as much as he wanted—even a whole pie if he felt like it. For the men working quite some distance from camp, the noon meal was hauled out by horses that were hitched to a dray. A big box was built on it especially for this purpose and everything was piping hot and wrapped in blankets. The lunch ground was prepared earlier in the fall. An area was cleared off and logs laid in a big square for the men to sit on. Inside the square, big bonfires were lit and the men ate in comfort. It wasn't quite as good as at camp, but then it took only a few minutes to wolf the food down. About 11:30 each morning the big Canadian jays and squirrels would start to gather around the lunch ground. It was quite a sight to see them fight over the cookies and doughnuts the men tossed to them. I think the men fed more to the birds and squirrels than they ate themselves.

In the main camp each bunkhouse had two big barrel stoves which the bull cook kept fired all the time during the winter months. On the stove in the rear was a big tub filled with hot water. Here the men could get water to wash and shave in the large wooden sink (with tin wash dishes) that stood in the corner of the room. Nearby was a large wooden barrel of cold water and a tin dipper hung by it. This was our drinking water and was also to be mixed with the hot water when washing face and hands. Everybody used the same towels. Every few days they were washed and clean ones were hung in place, but usually by spring one couldn't tell they had ever been washed.

The bunks were double deckers set end to end—two men in each bed, heads to heads, and feet to feet. Usually the men in the top bunks near the stove would just about suffocate from the heat while the men in the lower bunks down in the corner of the building would nearly freeze. This caused a lot of grumbling, but nothing more.

High above the stoves, wires were strung from one end of the bunkhouse to the other and this was where the men hung their wet mittens and socks at night—hundreds of pairs. What a sight!

BOREALIS

All in all the men were healthy from the long hours out in the cold fresh air and the good nourishing food, but they had to be tough. So many men sleeping in such crowded quarters, hundreds of pairs of stinking socks, and men passing gas all night was enough to give most men some kind of pox.

There was a table and two benches at the front end of each bunkhouse and here the men could play cards or sit and visit. The card games were usually whist or cribbage. There were many long, lonely nights on Isle Royale that winter, as we received no mail from home or news from the outside world. There were a few radios in camp but not in the bunkhouses.

The toilets were built quite a ways from the rear of the bunkhouses and were really primitive. They were about sixteen to twenty feet in length and about seven feet wide. To relieve themselves, the men had to sit on a pole with another pole behind them and a little higher for a back rest. In early days in lumber camps, the cooks would put something in the food to physic the men occasionally. They believed a good cleaning-out would prevent the men from catching cold or getting sick. I'm not sure this was what happened on Isle Royale one night. It could have been caused by the cooks not rinsing all the soap off the dishes. But the men were moved—and fast. About two o'clock in the morning I got the call and realized something was up, as there were men scurrying and cussing all over the place. When I got out there, every place was taken and some men were even sitting up on top of the back rests. How they held up, I'll never know, as the back rests were just toe-nailed into each end of the building. One poor old fellow just made it out the bunkhouse door and squatted down, when the next man out barrelled over him and knocked him over in the snow. As they came back inside, I heard some of the men saying "In the morning, I'm going to kill the cook, that S.O.B.!"

Sunday was the only day the lumberjack could call his own and this was the time he washed and patched his clothes. Usually down by a lake or creek fires were built under big iron kettles that were half full of water, and he made it a simple task because everything was tossed into the boiling water—wool shirts, socks, underwear, and mitten liners. After ten or fifteen minutes in the kettle, they were fished out with a stick and hung on a line, and in a short time they were frozen stiff. Later they were taken to the bunkhouse lines to dry. I've seen men throw underwear and bright red and black plaid wool shirts in the same water many times. By spring the underwear would be pink and the shirt a faded-out mess.

When the middle of April came, the snow was nothing more than slush as the weather became warmer. The men found their feet too hot in the rubbers they had worn all winter and soon changed to shoes. But this didn't work too well, as the dry shoes were like a wick and really got wet. I remember some of them conning the "cookees" into giving them "ole" to grease their shoes. They would split a pound of ole in two and put a half pound in each shoe—then put the shoes on. By night the ole was all melted and saturated the shoes from within. One old toothless jack I knew said, "I not only got my shoes greased, but when I took them off, I couldn't believe how clean my feet were!"

On the evening of April 24, 1936, the Coast Guard cutter *Crawford* came plowing into ice-covered Siskiwit Bay. They had come to take some of the men out and I was one of those who were leaving. Others had to stay to maintain the camp and get ready to put the pulp in the lake. But I vowed then that someday I would return to the old campsite at Siskiwit Bay. It took forty-two years, but I finally made it this July.

I'm glad I was a part of that camp because it was the beginning of the end of large-scale logging camps and lumberjacks. The next year (1936–1937)

18,000 cords of wood, summer of 1936.

51

BOREALIS

Everett Wynne ran a camp at Hovland for the George Mead Paper Company and it was his last of that type of logging.

Ranger Tim asked me who worked at the camp on Isle Royale. I told him "lumberjacks," and he asked "Did they have wives with them?" and I answered, "Lumberjacks didn't have wives. If they did, their wives had left them long ago." So he asked me to try to describe these men and I'll do my best.

They came in all sizes—from six-foot-four, two-hundred-forty pounders to some that didn't weigh over one hundred pounds soaking wet. But there was a job for them all and they did it well. As a group I don't think there ever was a better bunch of men as loyal to one another. They were hard-working and hard-drinking but they would go to the end of the earth to help a fellow worker out. As the saying goes—they would give the shirt off their backs. They are about all gone now—only a handful are left. I don't think there will ever be another bunch of men like them.

Today's woodsmen use different techniques and tools compared with the men of old. Of the tens of thousands that helped log Michigan, Wisconsin, and Minnesota, the majority of them never made over a dollar a day. There were a few exceptions—the four-horse teamster who probably made a dollar and a half; or good canthook men who specialized as top loaders in the days when logging sleds didn't have stakes. But they made money for the lumber barons who plundered and robbed untold millions of feet of lumber from these three states.

Most of the lumberjacks were immigrants who had come to this country seeking a new life and home. Many came from Sweden, Norway, and Finland; some from Canada; and of course many were U.S. citizens. Once a man was trapped in the lumberjack life it was very hard to get out. I remember two Finns I met on Isle Royale who told me how they had left their wives in Finland while they came to this country to earn enough money for passage for the rest of their families. They had come to find work on the Iron Range in Minnesota, but ended up working in the lumber camps. Twenty-five years passed and they said they could never make it past the Duluth "blind pigs." These men were in their middle fifties and still hoping that someday they would have enough money to bring their families to America. Who knows how often they had been shortchanged at the bars in all those years.

Usually a lumberjack could only work about two months at one time. Then he began to get itchy feet and a terrible thirst. After a week or so they were ready to come back to camp following their binge in the saloons and brothel. Then they couldn't be beat as workers. In the fall they bought the finest clothing—wool shirts, mackinaw pants (Sioux or Chippewa—the best brands), good lumberman's rubbers, and other clothing. These were charged against their wages, as there wasn't any cash. With patching and darning these clothes would last all winter. The jacks would look like scarecrows by spring after all this. When they drew all their wages they would head for town and in a matter of a few days (sometimes only a few hours) they would be broke. It was a common sight to have a jack yell "timber," and see men coming from all over to spear a free drink. Sometimes, if they got past the bar they would pay for a week's room and board at some cheap rooming house. Then they would hang around and bum until their luck ran out. Some of these men had good educations. Others had good singing voices and could have gone a long ways in the entertainment field.

In the early days traveling preachers called "Sky Pilots" would often visit camps, but they didn't have much influence on the men.

I was a farm boy and went to work in a camp for the first time when I was fifteen years old. Of course I was always with my Uncle Everett and when spring came, I went back home. But I've had many old jacks ask me if I had a home. When I told them I did, they all told me the same thing, "Go home, boy, and stay there."

I'm glad I had the opportunity to know and work with these fine men. As I said, they are almost all gone now and only a memory remains. I doubt we will ever see their likes again.

Christmas on Isle Royale

INTRODUCTION - *Few people celebrate Christmas on the Island and this is a rare account of one observance in the George Mead Company logging camp. This sketch comes from the park archives and its author is unknown. However, the tone of the account suggests it was written by a supervisor to prove that the loggers weren't suffering from lack of holiday cheer, or fellowship of men, or feminine graces.*

For most Island residents, isolation has only made them more determined to celebrate social events and holidays. Indeed, holiday events become more important on Isle Royale, as residents are cut off from family and mainland communities. Islanders' self-reliance extended from the work place to Christmas preparations. Those celebrating Christmas on Isle Royale (loggers, fishermen, trappers, and early copper miners) delighted in "pure and simple" pleasures made of native materials and on-the-spot creativity. Other gifts had to be ordered and hidden from prying eyes from the time of the last boat until Christmas.

For Island lumberjacks, Christmas was a welcome aberration from a six-day work week followed by a day of chores. Good health [there were no illnesses due to the isolation], "unequaled Christmas trees" (from a timberer's perspective), and a mix of Yankee and Scandinavian customs marked the Island celebration.

P ermit me to go back a few days or perhaps a few days longer before the holiday season, as an introduction as to who and why we are isolated here for the winter.

The George W. Mead Timber Operations, carrying on a lumber camp in the Siskiwit River valley, is cutting pulpwood to be rafted when navigation opens in the spring of 1936. The main camp is located at the mouth of the river and seventeen gangs of shackers [independent loggers] are up river. Time and space will not permit me to mention the entire personnel who are here, therefore just a few of the personnel will be named. This does not mean, however, that all are not equally important in their respective positions and just as essential toward making the project a complete success.

To name these few, Mr. Everett Wynne, foreman; Dr. Anthony Curreri, in charge of the hospital; Mr. J. S. Lindblom as supervisor; Mr. Ernest Sederberg as clerk; Mr. Sigurd Benson, Chef; Mr. Ellsworth St. Germain, in charge of Conservation and trapping of moose for the State of Michigan; Mrs. Curreri, Mrs. St. Germain, Mrs. Wynne, and little Dennis Wynne (7 months old); and 113 men, plus 75 to 80 men out in 17 shacks.

Navigation officially closed on December the 14th, when *Elmar the 2nd* sailed from here to Grand Marais, isolating us here until the spring of 1936. Our lumbering activities and the work of the Conservation men [Michigan Department of Conservation] will be over in the spring and we will all be leaving for our homes on the mainland again.

With our supplies here, enough to last for the season, radio equipment, reading material, and all other necessities and little luxuries, we are all well established for a nice, long, quiet winter. As far as contact with the outside world is concerned, we are like one large family, all working in peace and harmony to make it an interesting and agreeable stay for all.

A very pleasant surprise, and like a gift from the gods, what should sail into Siskiwit Bay on December 22nd, but the U.S. Coast Guard cutter *Crawford*, bringing us our Christmas mail, some medical supplies from the State of Michigan, and messages of good cheer from the mainland. Mr. Ransom, the Executive Officer, was in command of the vessel, Captain Egland being ill in a hospital in Chicago, which we were all very sorry to learn, and our prayers are for his speedy recovery. We were all very thankful for this pleasant surprise and all have the utmost respect and admiration for Mr. Ransom and his entire crew.

Having heard much about the unequaled Christmas trees on Isle Royale, they were all very anxious to have one, and their wishes were fulfilled as Mr. Wynne and Mr. Lindblom, with five of the ship's crew, went out with a team and brought in fifteen trees, which were as perfect as trees grow, and we all hope they will bring much good cheer to the entire crew and their friends.

Christmas being the most sacred of all our holidays and the season of the year when we should all rejoice, we were not to be left out of our share of the season's activities even though we were isolated. Entertainment was arranged for in our hospital "which we are very proud of." As yet we have had no cases of a serious nature or illness and sincerely hope that we will not have. However, we are well equipped to care for them and know that under Dr. and Mrs. Curreri's care they would have the very best of medical attention and care. Space would not permit the entire crew to attend the entertainment, therefore the members of the staff, hospital, kitchen, motive power [bulldozer and machine shop], and Conservation Dept. [there to trap and transplant moose] were all listed and the names of each person who was to attend was placed in a receptacle a few days before the entertainment. Each one drew a name and was requested to make a gift for the person whose name they drew, as there are no shops or stores on the Island where gifts could be purchased. Each one was to make the gift to be presented at the entertainment. Birchbark and wood played a greater part in the making of these gifts and the ingenuity shown in the skill and handiwork were most remarkable and many of these gifts will be treasured keepsakes long to be remembered and admired. Everyone made something and no one was left out. Everyone was presented with one of these fine articles when their names were called.

On Christmas Eve at 8 o'clock we all assembled at the hospital, twenty-four of us. Mrs. Curreri had the rooms decorated most beautifully. One of the unequaled Isle Royale Christmas trees stood in one corner of the living room, trimmed and decorated in the most elaborate fashion. The entire setting was one of fine taste and carried out the Christmas spirit and showed excellent skill in making a holiday festival complete. All the guests were seated in the living room. Mr. Lindblom appeared on the scene playing the part of Santa Claus, with a huge pack on his back containing the gifts that had been made. To make up the program for the entertainment, each recipient was requested to furnish a number or selection of some kind toward the program and everyone responded remarkably and every selection was excellent and appreciated. Time and space will not permit mentioning what each individual did or contributed; however, they were all worthy of mention. Some, however, I will mention: two vocal solos in Swedish by Mr. Oscar Nygren; violin solos by Mr. James Wynne and Mr. George Johnson, accompanied by Mr. Sigurd Benson on the bones; Thomas Melanson played very nicely on the harmonica; and when the gift was handed to little Dennis Wynne, he responded with one of his pleasing innocent smiles such as only a baby can smile.

In keeping with the occasion the entire group sang of Silent Night, Jingle Bells, and Come All Ye Faithful, led by Mrs. Curreri. There was prayer and scriptural reading by Mrs. St. Germain and a very fine reading by Mrs. Wynne.

At 11 o'clock a delicious lunch was served by Mrs. Curreri and Mrs. St. Germain. After lunch Mr. Johnson and Mr. Benson favored us with several musical selections on violin and bones. Mr. Nygren sang another Swedish song and several games were played, after which the radio played its part and we all enjoyed Midnight Mass. At an early hour we all departed, all unanimous in one opinion that Dr. and Mrs. Curreri are the perfect host and hostess and Christmas Eve had been a perfect one, and an inspiration to all.

Christmas morning dawned cloudy and with a light snowfall like all morn-ings on Isle Royale at this time of the year, but weather and snowfall did not come between us and a most perfect Christmas Day, or as nearly so as possible away from immediate families and loved ones. Mr. Lindblom started the day by bringing to the Island an old Swedish custom "Kaffe pa sangen" [coffee in bed], commonly in Sweden called "Jul Bokken" [Christmas treats in the morn-ing] to the three families.

At 9:30 A.M. Central Standard Time, radio station WHDF of Calumet, Michigan, broadcast a special program for the people of Isle Royale, which was highly appreciated. Special messages were sent to Mr. and Mrs. St. Germain by friends and to our wireless operator, Mr. Louis Baranowski, by his father and mother, who reside at Calumet. Also messages were broadcast to the Holger Johnson family at Chippewa Harbor.

All the shackers were invited to camp for a dinner of turkey with all the trimmings. Any word by mouth or pen could not describe or improve on that dinner prepared by Mr. Benson and his efficient staff. Candy for all was served by Mr. and Mrs. St. Germain. Apples were given out by Mr. Wynne and Mr. Sederberg and cigars by Dr. Curreri and Mr. Lindblom. All the shackers seemed to enjoy the radio programs and all the radios in camp, of which six were in use to bring good cheer to all who wished to listen to them. Open house prevailed everywhere and the Spirit of Christmas was with all, and everybody had a most wonderful day.

Dinner being over most of the crew and shackers spent time visiting. Some went skiing or snowshoeing. Mr. Underwood and Mr. Lindblom went snowshoeing there [to isolated shackers] delivering parcels left for them by Santa Claus the night before.

Mrs. Wynne had a most beautiful tree, elaborately decorated for little Dennis, and their cabin was decorated with wreaths and decorations which carried out the holiday spirit and greetings to all who entered there. Mrs. St. Germain also had a very fine tree well decorated and their cabin was an inspiration of the holiday season. Mrs. Wynne and Mrs. St. Germain presented the office and kitchen staffs with beautiful wreaths for the office and kitchen windows, which added to the Christmas cheer to both places and were highly appreciated.

In conclusion I will say it was a Christmas we will all remember as a most pleasant one for all of us, and we owe many thanks to Mrs. Curreri and Mrs. St. Germain for their work and efforts in making it a Merry Christmas for all.

Historic Mining

INTRODUCTION - *Written in 1965, Prof. Lawrence Rakestraw's "Historic Mining on Isle Royale" is an example of enduring
scholarship. "Historic Mining" is thorough and exacting, yet easy
reading. Little can be added to this record, except for what the
years have erased and what a newer perspective might add. Today
there are fewer remains of the three mining periods on the Island.
The logging dam at the Minong Mine operation gave way and re-
maining log structures continue to melt into the ground. Remnants of one of the first
copper smelters in the Upper Great Lakes lies forgotten near Daisy Farm. The copper
mining legacy remains though it is more subtle, such as the exotic plants—alfalfa,
clover, timothy and others—brought by miners to feed their livestock, stamp sands
sporting fireweed, and a fire-altered forest canopy.*

*Centuries of legends of a copper island fired miners' dreams and hopes of finding
a mother lode on Isle Royale. For some, this dream was more compelling than bad
news of copper veins which "pinched out" and investments which bore little economic
return. Successive teams of miners came to the Island frontier; unfortunately, we
know little about their daily thoughts, their trials and tribulations.*

*Recently uncovered manuscripts tell us of itinerant priests who sojourned to the
Island to minister to the miners' spiritual needs. Further, Island copper miners were
not absolutely alone. Miners met and traded with visiting Ojibwa who made moccasins and caught fish for White trade goods. Schooners and steamers also brought the
mail, and Victorian-age tourists and investors occasionally came. Mining conditions on the Island were primitive and miners labored heroically to win copper from
the rock.*

THE EARLIEST MINERS - Copper mining on Isle Royale is no recent
thing—in fact it has spanned a period of more than 4,500 years. When man

first arrived in the New World, perhaps 15,000 to 20,000 years ago, Isle Royale was still covered with thick glacial ice. By the time the ice receded from the Lake Superior Basin and Isle Royale rose above the waters of the lake about 10,000 years ago, Indians already had begun to occupy parts of the Upper Great Lakes.

It will never be known when the first man ventured out across Lake Superior to Isle Royale, but by 2,500 B.C. or shortly thereafter, Indians began to exploit the pure copper deposits that were exposed on the surface of the Island. Archeologists feel that the Indians may not have deliberately prospected for copper, at least at first, but in the course of their travels about the Island, they would watch for nuggets and veins of the bright metal. Eventually a method was developed of extracting the raw copper from the bedrock by beating it free with rounded, hand-held beach cobbles. Thus, numerous pits were dug in the most productive locations on the Island, especially along Minong Ridge. Recent archeological excavations have uncovered large numbers of hammerstones from the ancient mines which are now filled in by soil and covered with vegetation.

More than 1,000 pits attributed to the Indians have been located on Isle Royale, but since the activity covered a period of at least 1,500 years, there is no basis for suggesting any highly organized efforts to procure the copper. Rather, the mining probably was pursued in the course of an annual round of hunting, fishing, and collecting berries and plants. The copper itself was cold-hammered into knives, points, and a variety of ornaments, either on Isle Royale or after being taken to the mainland. Artifacts of Lake Superior copper ultimately made their way to the southern Lake States and New England. Unfortunately, very little is known about the way of life of these earliest miners, since no habitation sites from the mining period have been located on Isle Royale.

A fuller description of the Indian visits is left to another writer. This booklet narrates the chapters of more recent mining activity, starting in the 1840s and ending at the turn of the century.

HISTORIC MINING - Mining frontiers in the United States have followed a common pattern. Historically, they have been important in that they often brought the first permanent white population to isolated or uninviting areas. They have typically begun by a discovery or rumors of precious metal. Mining of a simple type led to the establishment of settlements, roads, and other facilities. Dwindling deposits often caused an equally rapid decline in population, with perhaps a few of the better-financed companies staying on. As time went on, a very different type of mining would develop based on the use of heavy machinery and the advice of trained mining engineers and geologists. Eventually, in most areas, the deposits played out, and tourism or ranching replaced the mining.

Isle Royale followed this pattern in many ways. There was an early boom-and-bust period, lasting from 1843 to 1855; a lull, and then a revival of mining activity from 1873 to 1881; again a decline, and then a final flurry of mining from 1889 to 1893, ending with a shift to tourism and commercial fishing. Yet Isle Royale is also unique among mining frontiers in several respects. The linking of prehistoric mining with the recent era established a far longer time interval in mining history than on other frontiers; fishing and tourism played a greater and earlier part as supplementary economic activities; and the area, in its final stages, attracted large foreign investment.

Production of Isle Royale Mines

Mine	Years	Production (lbs. refined copper)
Siskowit Mine	1847–1855	190,736
Pittsburg & I.R.	1847–1853	27,730
Saginaw Mine	1875–1879	51,264
Island Mine	1874–1878	213,245
Minong Mine	1874–1883	498,650

THE FIRST MINING FRONTIER

The first mining explorations on Isle Royale began in 1843, after the Chippewa Indians relinquished claim to the Island under a treaty of the previous year. Previously the only white men living on the Island were seasonal fishermen, using the fish houses erected by the American Fur Company between 1837 and 1841. A few mineral locations were filed in 1843 under permit from the War Department; however, the main rush did not begin until 1846, partly because of the more accessible deposits on the mainland, partly because of an erroneous belief that mining rights under the existing mining laws did not extend beyond the south shore of Lake Superior. In 1846, however, a rush began that reached its peak the following year, then rapidly declined and came to an end in 1855.

The presence of copper on Isle Royale was a matter of common knowledge by 1843, with information ranging from Jesuit accounts and tales of American Fur Company fishermen to formal geological reports. To this impetus could be added the boom spirit of the time, an abundance of venture capital, and a highly unrealistic estimate of the ease by which fortunes could be acquired through copper mining. One 1846 guide to the mines presented a commonly held belief.

> The cost of getting ore to the surface, on Lake Superior, is about four dollars per ton, one hand being able to get out about half a ton per day. The cost of smelting or washing, so far, is about half that price—say altogether about six dollars per ton. If the ore yield 25% of metal, it is worth, at sixteen cents a pound, eighty dollars; thus leaving a large margin for profits, after paying the expenses of working the mines.

Mining operations were carried on by stock companies incorporated in various states—New York, Vermont, Ohio, Michigan, and Illinois were among those represented. At least a dozen such companies had locations on Isle Royale in 1847. The companies varied a great deal—some having professional geologists or mining engineers as agents and advisors, and a respectable amount of capital; others poor in everything except hope and courage; and still others that apparently existed only to sell stock.

Prospecting was simplicity itself. A promising fissure or contact vein or dike would be located, sometimes from a boat, sometimes by burning off the vegetation to expose the bedrock. The vein would be followed up, with miners excavating and blasting as they went along, and if the prospects looked promising a shaft would be sunk. As a result, in addition to the established mines, there are hundreds of sites where such explorations are evident. The mining locations were spread around the periphery of the Island, like beads on a string, from Malone Bay to Rock Harbor and around to Washington Harbor.

THE MINERS - Workers were divided into surface men and miners. The surface men worked above ground for wages of about a dollar a day. They cut timber, erected machinery, cleared land, set up tramways, and moved waste rock. Their usual costume consisted of heavy leather boots, canvas trousers, red flannel shirts, and low-crowned, broad-brimmed hats. Of special importance among this group was the blacksmith, whose job it was to sharpen drills and repair metal work.

The miners, on the other hand, worked on a contract basis of so much per foot dug. In the Siskowit silver mine at McCargoe Cove, for example, the miners got $20.00 per fathom. Out of this, however, they paid for their supplies—black powder, fuse (at $2.50 per five hundred feet), and tallow candles (15¢ per pound). The drills, however, were sharpened at company expense. In charge of each operation was an agent, or superintendent, who directed surface operations and made contracts and purchases. Below ground a mining captain was boss.

Many of the mining locations consisted of only one or two log cabins. The more substantial settlements—those at Ransom, Siskowit Mine, Snug Harbor, and Todd Harbor—followed a standard pattern. The agent resided in a house of squared logs, while miners lived in crude log cabins. At the Siskowit Mine, in addition, a dozen single workers lived in a combination storehouse and barracks. The grass and vegetation around the settlements was burned to keep accidental fires from destroying the place. Vegetable gardens of potatoes, peas, lettuce, and radishes were grown at Snug Harbor, Ransom, and Siskowit Mine, while the Siskowit operation had extensive hay pastures for their horses. Fish, potatoes, and tea were staples of the miners' diet, supplemented with beef brought in from the mainland.

The sparse population of the Island reached a peak of about 120 in the summer of 1847. Most of the men were evacuated each winter, leaving only a skeleton work force.

Life was hazardous, with many injuries and deaths due to drowning, mine accidents, or sheer lack of medical attention. C. G. Shaw in his diary tells of attacks of piles and dysentery, a toothache cured by rather drastic home dentistry, and an accident in which he nearly cut off his great toe. If this weren't enough, he was nearly blinded by bites from mosquitoes and black flies, nagged by the women in camp, and had to put up with insubordination from his Irish workmen! Yet there were compensations. Fishing, rock collecting, and visiting other mines were the chief forms of recreation, and the arrival of the mail boat was always a red-letter day. Trails were built between locations, notably between Ransom and McCargoe Cove, from Siskowit Mine to Malone Bay, from Washington Harbor to Huginnin Cove, and from Huginnin Cove to Todd Harbor. However, most travel was by water.

BOREALIS

MINE OPERATION - Copper was classified in the Lake Superior country in three grades according to its state of occurrence in the rock: "mass," "barrel work," and "stamp." Masses were large sheets of pure copper occurring in the vein, and weighing from a few hundred pounds to many tons. Smaller masses were taken from the mine intact; larger chunks were divided by means of chiseling. Barrel-work consisted of smaller pieces of copper in bundles and string-like form, bound together with veinstone—the worthless rocky material in the ore bearing vein. With these, as much of the adhering rock as possible was picked free with a hammer, and the copper was barreled up in casks holding from 500 to 800 pounds. Stamp copper consisted of pebble-sized or smaller pieces of metallic copper bound in rock which had to be pulverized by stamping. In this process, the ore was first roasted to make the veinstone friable, so it would yield to the blows of the stamps. The stamp mills consisted of a series of heavy metal shoes, operating from a cam shaft driven by water or steam power. The shoes would crush the ore, and the metal would be separated from the copper through a series of washings.

Most of the copper shipped from Isle Royale—the ore was taken down the lake to Sault Ste. Marie, and thence across to the lower lakes to be smelted—was mass or barrel work. Only two stamp mills operated on the Island during this first frontier.

The underground workings consisted of vertical shafts about six feet by eight feet sunk to a suitable depth—generally about sixty feet—where stoping would begin, that is, excavation of the ore made accessible by the shaft. Black powder was used to loosen rock and aid in excavating. The miners, dressed in canvas trousers and stout boots, with candles held on their hard hats by means of a lump of clay, would descend into the mine by ladder, and work an eight- or ten-hour shift. Rock was hoisted out by means of wooden ore buckets. Hand windlasses were used to hoist the ore to the surface in smaller operations; in the more substantial mines hand work was superseded by horse-powered hoists.

Ventilation and water were the two major problems of mining. The black powder fumes polluted the air, already foul as the shaft grew deeper. To combat this it was a common practice to dig a drift or "winze"—a horizontal tunnel— to another shaft. Water was always troublesome. Where the terrain was favorable, horizontal tunnels (adits) were dug from the surface to connect with the shaft and drain surface water. In the deeper mines steam pumps had to be used.

Most of the mining prospects in the '40s and '50s were short-lived and of little importance. Four, however, are significant.

*Early drill rig on Isle Royale, used to examine the
structure of the bedrock ca. 1892.*

Smithwick Mine

The Smithwick Mine was one of the earliest established on Isle Royale and is probably the one most often seen by visitors today. It was located in July 1843 by James Smithwick and worked by his agent, C. G. Shaw. Active work began in 1847, when a blacksmith shop, a root cellar, and several dwellings were built, some near the mine, some just to the east of the present Rock Harbor marina. Two shafts were started, and a great deal of exploration in the vicinity was carried on. By 1848 the main shaft had been sunk to the depth of 90 feet. Little copper was found, and we have no record of commercial production. The present remains of the prospect consist of four shafts, on a north-south line, along the Moose Trail leading from Snug Harbor.

Ohio and Isle Royale

The Ohio and Isle Royale Company, like the Siskowit, was given permission by the Secretary of War to file on Isle Royale locations between Rock Harbor and Chippewa Harbor. A townsite named Ransom, after the agent, Leander Ransom, was soon established. In 1847, forty or fifty men cleared land, built houses, planted a garden, and explored on the ridge north of the townsite for copper. Early prospects looked promising, and a smelter was built that year.

The venture was short-lived. The smelter was poorly constructed and did not work satisfactorily; their explorations did not prove rich enough in copper to justify working, and in 1849 the company left the Island and located just east of Houghton on Portage Lake. Fire destroyed the mining buildings at Ransom in 1866. Ransom was subsequently the site of a sawmill, a garden supplying vegetables for Rock Harbor Lodge, and a CCC Camp, and today is the location of Daisy Farm Lakeside Camp.

Pittsburg and Isle Royale

This company, incorporated in Pittsburgh about 1846, began its mining activities in 1847 in the Todd Harbor area. In that year two log cabins and a blacksmith shop were erected, and nine men worked on a shaft near the shore. The following year they made other explorations, mostly near the shore, but one about a mile south of the shore. Here they reached a depth of 225 feet and then found the pumps unable to cope with the water. By 1849 they struck profitable veins, mostly mass and barrel-work, near the lake and later had 25 men employed and a stamp mill under construction. Their last year of recorded production was 1853; they apparently closed operations because of the isolated location and lack of protection from northerly gales.

Siskowit Mining Company

This company went through a series of early changes, beginning as the Isle Royale Union Company in 1844, reorganizing as the Siskowit Mining Association in 1847, and becoming the Siskowit Mining Company in 1849. For our purposes we can consider these companies as the same. In its final form it was incorporated in Michigan, with directors from Washington, D.C., Wisconsin, and Philadelphia, and had Charles Whittlesey, an eminent geologist and businessman, as agent. Preliminary explorations were carried on in 1844, but little was done until 1846. In that year the company established headquarters in an old fishing cabin (possibly remaining from the American Fur Company venture) across from Mott Island. The agent, together with his work force of a blacksmith, a carpenter, and two laborers, explored Mott and Outer Hill islands. They excavated 600 pounds of rock, discarded 200, stamped the rest with the aid of a beach boulder and a swing pole, and recovered rock having 15% copper in it.

But soon they abandoned this location for a more promising one on the main island. During the winter they sank a shaft in a vein of chlorite and epidote near the cabin and about 80 yards from the shore. The next year they blanketed the north shore with locations from Washington Harbor to McCargoe Cove, in many cases taking over prospects abandoned by other companies. Of these north shore locations only one proved to be profitable, a combination silver and copper mine near McCargoe Cove. They excavated a drift here for sixty feet and began stoping, recovering some silver and copper; but this mine seems to have been abandoned by 1849.

By 1850 work centered in the Rock Harbor location across from Mott Island. The settlement soon included a large hewed log house for the agent, numerous shanties for the workers and their families, and a log storehouse with barracks in it for a dozen single men. A steam stamp mill was set up in 1850 with water obtained from the lake by means of a large Cornish pump. The original vein was abandoned for another about 200 yards to the north and east, where a long adit was dug to lake level for drainage, and several shafts sunk along the vein. The deepest reached 360 feet.

The original plan had been to send the ore by flatboat two miles down the harbor to the Ohio and Isle Royale Smelter, but this failed. One load was

69

shipped and smelted, but as Charles Whittlesey remarked, "The product therefrom, either from some defect in the furnace or want of skill in running the smelter, was only 2670 pounds of badly smelted copper." Later loads were shipped down the lake to the smelters in Cleveland or Detroit.

In the winter of 1852–1853 the stamp mill burned. The whole work force then took to the woods, cut timber, and had it hauled to the mine site by the only horse on the Island, an animal that was old, blind, and lame. There saw pits were set up, the timber whipsawed by hand, and a new mill was ready for installation of machinery by spring.

The Siskowit prospered for some time, producing 190,736 pounds of refined copper between 1847 and 1855. But the geology of the site worked against the venture. The upper stratum of rock was rich in masses, barrel stock, and stamp copper, but it dipped toward the lake. Consequently the miners, in order to get at the largest bodies of ore, had to excavate under the lake, and more water came in than the pumps could handle. Beneath this stratum was a hard layer of basaltic rock in which the vein pinched out. These factors, coupled with financial difficulties, caused the mine to close in 1855.

END OF THE BOOM - The mining boom came to an end as rapidly as it had started. By the end of 1847 about half of the companies that had been in operation the earlier part of the year were closed. By 1850 only two companies were in operation, and in 1855 the last of these companies closed up. There were a variety of reasons for this collapse of the boom. A change of the mining law, from lease on a royalty basis to sale, was made in 1847, which forced many of the marginal or speculative enterprises to cease operations.

The isolation of the Island placed it at a disadvantage to the mainland operations. Above all, however, was the fact that the stamp rock on Isle Royale was not very rich in copper, and only by producing masses and barrel work could the mines have prospered.

THE SECOND MINING FRONTIER

The period between 1855 and 1871 was marked by a lull in mining activities. No mines operated during this time, and the Island was uninhabited save by fishermen who, during the summer, occupied the old American Fur Company houses in the Siskiwit Bay area and on Fish Island. In summer, visitors came over at frequent intervals on vessels ranging from Mackinaw boats to excursion steamers carrying up to 200 passengers. They picnicked in the clover fields at the Siskowit Mine site, fished, and enjoyed the Island much as visitors do today.

But the Civil War needs for metal soon caused a rise in the price of copper at a time when national land laws were favorable for speculative buying at low cost. The North American Mineral Land Company—closely connected with the Quincy Mining Company in Hancock, Michigan—began buying up the Island, first by use of Connecticut state agricultural college scrip and later by direct purchase at $1.25 an acre. Soon they had purchased 70,000 acres, their holdings including most of the Island outside the sandstone belt south of Siskiwit Bay. Their original intention was to revive the operations in the Rock Harbor, Todd Harbor, and Huginnin Cove areas, and to this end they corresponded with former mining captains who had worked in those sites. In 1871 they sent explorers to the Island. As a result of their reports three new mining ventures began, one to the north and two on the south side of the Island.

In these three undertakings we find much that is common to the second stage of the mining frontier. Trained mining engineers and geologists with a new technique—diamond drilling—supplemented the old haphazard search for outcrops. With more reliable and regular transportation by lake steamer the settlements enjoyed more amenities of life. Schools were established in all the later settlements; physicians and clergymen were represented in the population. The population makeup also changed. Except for the Siskowit Mine, which used Cornishmen, the labor force in the earlier mines had been Americans, Germans, or Irish. After 1870, other nationalities appeared, and specialization took place. Cornish miners migrated to Isle Royale, as they did to all parts of the Copper Country, and took over the underground activity. Finns and Norwegians were used as wood crews, and Germans and Irishmen as laborers. The new mining ventures had close financial ties with mining interests on the mainland, particularly with the Quincy interests.

Minong Mine

Near Minong Ridge in the McCargoe Cove area are hundreds of pits left by Indians who had mined for copper masses. These pits attracted the early attention of miners, and in 1874 three companies were formed in Detroit to exploit them—The Minong, the Cove and the Ancient Mining companies. Of these three only the Minong was active; but the companies were essentially the same, since they had virtually the same officers and the same board of

71

directors. The Minong Company obtained title from the North American Mineral Land Company to 1,455 acres along Minong Ridge. A year later they acquired the 1,190 acres of the Cove Company. With these holdings, virtually all the land between Lake Superior and Chickenbone Lake and west to Todd Harbor, was in their hands. S. W. Hill, who had been in charge of the exploring companies, described the possibilities in glowing terms. Abundant timber, he said, was available and well located; one road would command all the veins; and the old Indian workings would serve as guides to the best bodies of ore.

Work began in earnest in 1875. A substantial dock and warehouse were built at the mouth of McCargoe Cove, where lake steamers could unload goods and load copper ore. A tug and flat boats were used to transport goods through the narrow Z-shaped entrance to the cove and up two miles to the mine settlement. On September ninth Alonzo C. Davis, the agent, wrote, "The past three days have been big copper days for Minong." During this time they had taken out one mass weighing 6,000 pounds, another of 3,500–4,000 pounds, and still another of 2,500–3,000 pounds, besides much barrel stock and stamp copper. A wagon road had been built from the shore to the mining area and a railroad started, with about 600 feet of track laid at each end. Six dwellings had been completed in addition to a store and an office building. Fifty men were employed.

That winter was a hard one, with too much ice for boats and not enough for travel over the ice. Directors of the company, who had expected to have regular mail service by way of Pigeon River, became alarmed over the lack of communication—so alarmed, indeed, that one director tried to get in touch with Davis through a medium. "Madame Blank" duly obliged with tales of large production in copper and silver. It is unlikely that Davis appreciated this attempted communication; his letters show him to have been a crusading agnostic! By May, however, Davis could report that the colony was still alive. During the winter they had taken out thirty tons of mass and barrel work, and a large pile of stamp rock. The population had remained static: two men had drowned in trying to carry mail to the mainland, and two children had been born.

There followed flush years for the Minong, with high production. Though two shafts were sunk, one to a depth of 300 feet, most of the work was a quarrying operation by means of open pits. A stamp mill was built, powered by steam and obtaining water from a 12-foot high log dam on a tributary to Chickenbone Creek. A railroad led from the dock to the mine site; a spur of the railroad ran to the stamp mill, and another from the stamp mill to the ore dock. The blacksmith, with his shop located at the mine itself, must have been in great demand to shoe the many horses needed in hauling ore cars from the excavations to the railroad loading platforms and to repair the metal machinery. As the mining settlement grew, a schoolmaster was hired. Prosperity and a demand for self-government led to the establishment of Isle Royale County, with the county seat at Island Mine and the Minong settlement of Cove as a separate township.

By 1879, however, production began to fall off. Some of the difficulties were due to poor management, but more to poor rock. So long as large masses were available the mine prospered; but the stamp rock, about 1½% copper, could not be stamped and transported profitably. As the *Ontonagon Herald* remarked, "The ancients got the juice and left us moderns little but the acrid rind to nibble at." From 1881 to 1883 it was let on tribute—that it, leased for a share of the proceeds—and by 1885 it closed completely.

Island Mine

On the south side of the Island an equally ambitious but shorter-lived operation grew up. S. W. Hill's party discovered a large number of Indian pits to the north of Siskiwit Bay. The Island Mining Company was organized in 1873, and that fall a force of 80 men reported for work on the Island. With over 400,000 board-feet of lumber shipped to the Island, they laid out a town-site on the north side of Siskiwit Bay and built a road two miles to the mine. The group passed the first winter without incident. On March 19, 1874 two men wrote to the *Portage Lake Mining Gazette* from the settlement:

> Rev. Father Baxter, Jesuit missionary, arrived from Silver Islet yesterday, accompanied by three men, leaving there the day before. Today the reverend gentleman is busy among the Catholic population. He reports the ice strong, and thinks a horse team could cross with safety between here and Silver Islet. A number of people have crossed on the ice this year to visit us. It seems strange owing to the fact that the weather has been reasonably mild and pleasant; still, the ice is strong. We are not so isolated after all. Our people are all well and in good spirits. There has not been a single case of sickness, nor one injured at the mine. Four men met with an accident while quarrying rock at the dock last fall, but they are all out now. Everybody seems to be contented, and there has not been a single breach of peace since close of navigation. This is not bad for a population of 130 people.
>
> Yours truly,
> Pick and Gad

A mining family at Windigo.

During the next two years ambitious plans were carried out. Three shafts were opened, ultimately reaching depths of 50, 150, and 200 feet, the deeper ones connected with one another by drifts. A village was built at the mine location, a large hoist was hauled in, and a stone powder house constructed at Senter Point. A sawmill was set up, probably at the mouth of Caribou Creek. Original plans had been to build a stamp mill by the shore, to flume water down from a dam near the mine site, and to build a railroad from the mine site to the stamp mill. However, only part of this was accomplished. A massive earth-fill dam was constructed, and a railroad bed laid down as far as the creek on which the dam was located. Then came a series of disasters. The dock and warehouse burned in 1874, and the fire swept nearly up to the mining location. The price of copper fell. Investors lost confidence. On September 23, 1875, the *Portage Lake Mining Gazette* reported that all work on the Island Mine had ceased. The conglomerate, rich enough near the surface, had become poorer at greater depths; and the lode was "bunchy." The company cancelled contracts for lumber and stamp mill machinery, and all available supplies, including the tug *Maythorn*, were offered for sale. One man was left as caretaker for the village.

Tributors worked the mine for three years, doing some stoping, but largely using the rock already excavated. They built a small stamp mill on a creek near the mine location, using for water and transportation the dam and railroad already in place, but they, too, were beset with frustrations, including the burning of their mill. It was not long before they had abandoned the place. In 1881 Alexander Winchell, the Minnesota state geologist, found the buildings and machinery still on the shore, but soon thereafter the warehouse burned, and today the townsite shows no signs of its former occupancy.

Saginaw Mine

Still a third operation took place, this to the south of Conglomerate Bay, near Rock Harbor. The Saginaw Mining Company, apparently backed by Marquette capital, sent out a small work force in 1877 to mine an old location formerly prospected by the Ohio and Isle Royale Company. They sank two shafts with a winze connecting them and took out a limited amount of copper. But operations ceased after 1879.

FINAL EXPLORATIONS

Isle Royale Land Corporation

With the closing of these mines the Island again remained uninhabited save for seasonal fishermen. The North American Mineral Land Company, aware that it had a bad investment on its hands, sought to dispose of its holdings and hired Jacob Houghton, a brother of Douglass Houghton, to do the job. Jacob Houghton, who ran a shipping line from Hancock to Isle Royale, was a curious mixture of Micawber and Pollyanna whose faith in Isle Royale copper had lasted for forty years. This was a period in which the British were making large investments in American mines, and he finally succeeded in interesting a Liverpool syndicate in his copper dream. They took the name of the Isle Royale Land Corporation and purchased the holding of the North American Mineral Land Company as well as the Minong interests (about 84,000 acres) for about three dollars an acre. While emphasizing the value of the copper, Houghton also stressed the land itself as an investment. He demonstrated his faith by buying 800 of the 10,000 shares.

Wendigo Copper Company

The charter of the Isle Royale Land Corporation permitted them to explore for copper but not to mine it, and actual mining was needed to prove values. Therefore, a subsidiary company, the Wendigo Copper Company (the company used an "e" in their spelling of Windigo), was founded, and eight thousand acres set aside for it in the Washington Harbor area. Here, at the present Windigo development, grew up the Island's most elaborate townsite, Ghyllbank. A huge log office building was constructed; store houses and sheds grew up along the shore; while two miles inland the mining location settlement, "Wendigo," was constructed. It consisted of a number of one- or two-story log cabins built for workers on the location and two boarding houses for the single men.

The mining community numbered about 135, of whom only sixty were men. There were at least twenty children of school age, and some pre-school children, including two infants born during the winter of 1890–1891. The physician was both school teacher and customs officer. Tobogganing was a favorite sport during the winter, with an excellent toboggan slide from the office building down the hill to the ice on the bay; at night the slide was lit by lanterns. Mail service was regular, by way of Pigeon River carried by boats in summer and dog teams in winter, and there were few of the hardships that had marked the earlier settlements.

From 1890 to 1892 there was frenzied activity. Many miles of road were built in the Washington Harbor area and as far inland as Lake Desor. Much trenching was done to discover the nature of the bedrock in this area, as well as in Todd Harbor, and an extensive program of diamond drill exploration was carried out. (Incidentally, these rock cores gives us our best knowledge of the geology of the Island today.) But all this resulted in no production of copper. The rock was too poor to be mined profitably. In 1892 the activity ceased, the Wendigo company went out of existence, and the Isle Royale Land Corporation began selling its land for tourist homes and resorts.

At this time the *Engineering and Mining Journal* editorialized:

> This ends the last attempt to find a mine on Isle Royale. It is probable that a million dollars has been spent on this island in fruitless explorations, made by practical men with their own money, and not by stock companies. It may safely be said that there are no paying deposits on the island.

THE END OF AN ERA

Historic mining on Isle Royale was a colorful episode in the history of the Island. In general, the activity paralleled the story of other mining frontiers in the United States, with its cycles of boom and decline, and, at a later period, in the application of science and technology to the operations. The large foreign investment in the last period of development is typical of the mining frontiers of the far west. In the west, urban centers such as Fort Benton, Spokane, and San Francisco served as supply centers for the isolated mining areas. On Isle Royale, Houghton and Duluth played similar roles, with lake steamers and tugs taking the place of the western freight wagons and pack mules. As in the West, a period came in the twentieth century when men found it more profitable to work tourists than ore bodies. The transition of Aspen, Colorado, from a silver mining center to a haven for philosophers and skiers took about forty years. On Isle Royale the transition was more rapid, with the end of the mining era coinciding with the beginning of tourism as a major economic activity.

THE REMAINS TODAY

Visible remains of the fifty years of mining ventures on the Island are still plentiful, and most of the sites are accessible by trail. "Poor rock" piles, the debris from shafts and excavations, are evident wherever a mine existed. Closer investigation of the larger mine sites will reveal the eroded foundations of houses, stamp mills, and storehouses.

At Rock Harbor you can see the shaft holes from the old Smithwick Mine along the Moose Trail leading from the Lodge, and a hike of 4½ miles will take you to the largest mine development in the Harbor, the Siskowit site. At Windigo, early exploration trenches are identified along the Windigo Nature Trail, while decaying log structures dating from the Wendigo Mine operations are within easy hiking distance from the campground.

The two greatest mine developments are inland, but also reached by trails. From the McCargoe Cove Lakeside Camp take the Mine Trail to explore the digging site where 50 men once were employed, and follow the old railroad part way down from the mine. In the same vicinity look for foundations of the long-gone stamp mill, less than a quarter of a mile from the campground on the Chickenbone Lake Trail. Vestiges of the Island Mine are seen along the trail of that name leading off the Greenstone Ridge.

The National Park Service plans to identify many of these original mining sites, install interpretive exhibits, and make them available to Park visitors. In the meantime, you may visit these areas but you should remember that structures remaining from the old mining operations are fragile and easily damaged.

77

Their loss would be disastrous to future plans. Look, photograph, and enjoy, but do not disturb.

The timbers of the old shafts and stopes have long since rotted, and the interiors are unsafe. **Never enter one of these excavations.** Some of the shafts are unmarked and surrounded by undergrowth. Use care in your explorations.

BIBLIOGRAPHIC NOTES & ACKNOWLEDGMENTS

I wish to express my thanks to Calumet and Hecla, Inc., for giving me access to their large file on Isle Royale mines in their Calumet office. Valuable manuscript material on these mines was found in the National Archives, the Detroit Public Library, and the Michigan Historical Collections in Ann Arbor. Mrs. Ruth Gray of Ann Arbor and Mr. Edgar Johns of Duluth gave me first-hand information on the Wendigo operations. The National Park Service file on the Wendigo Copper Company, and the back files of the *Portage Lake Mining Gazette* at Michigan Technological University, both proved useful. The field notes and plates of the 1847 survey by William Ives were indispensable for the field work involved in this study.

It will be possible to mention only a small number of the books and articles used in this study. Charles T. Jackson, *Report on the Geological and Mineralogical Survey of the Mineral Lands of the United States in the State of Michigan* (31st Cong. 1st Sess., Exec. Doc. 5, Washington, 1849), gives a fair account of the early mines. Of greater importance is Alfred C. Lane, *Geological Report on Isle Royale* (Michigan Geological Survey, Vol. 6, Pt. 1, Lansing, 1898). Statistics on production are from B. S. Butler and W. S. Birbank, *The Copper Deposits of Michigan* (U.S. Geological Survey Prof. Paper 144, Washington, 1929). The technical journals in the Michigan Technological University library contain much useful information.

Charlie & Angelique Mott

INTRODUCTION - *The drama of Charlie and Angelique Mott's sufferings in 1845 on remote Isle Royale is a classic tale. Hazy rumors of Indian use of the Island, and especially prehistoric copper mining, give way to this epic which chronicles themes of abandonment, hardship, mistrust, native ingenuity, and stamina. The Mott legend helped characterize 19th-century Isle Royale as a place where fears of abandonment and starvation were very real. The theme of Island abandonment lingers in some hearts and minds, but is no longer a pervasive concern.*

The story of Charlie and Angelique Mott was, and remains, popular. Its popularity can be charted by its different versions; over eleven different tellings have been recorded. It is clearly a hybrid of Ojibwa and Euro-American stories. Ojibwa "windigo" stories which chronicle the effects of mid-winter stress and hunger are integrated with Euro-American concerns of Christianity, morality, and possessing frontier resources. The legend is also a story of transitions from a native to white viewpoint and dominance on the Island. It is the only story which personalizes the Indian presence on Isle Royale. But perhaps most remarkably it is also a story about feminine inner strength and the weaknesses of men.

"When I and my husband Charlie Mott were first married we lived at LaPointe. Mr. Douglas, Mr. Barnard, and some other 'big bugs' from Detroit had come up there in the schooner *Algonquin*, looking for copper. From LaPointe, Charlie and I went over with them, on their invitation, to Isle Royale. After landing with the rest, I wandered a long way on the beach until I saw something shining in the water. It was a piece of mass copper. When I told the *Algonquin* people of it they were very glad and determined at once to locate it. They said if Charlie and I would occupy it for them, Charlie should have $25 a month and I $5 a month to cook for him. Having agreed to the bargain, we returned to the Sault to lay in a good supply of provisions. There, I first met Mendenhall, the man who brought us into all this trouble. He said there was no need of carrying provisions so far up the lake, and at so heavy an expense, as he had plenty of provisions at LaPointe. When we got to LaPointe, we found that this was not so. All we could get was a half barrel of flour (which we had to borrow from the mission), six pounds of butter that smelled bad and was white like lard, and a few beans. I didn't want to go the Island until we had something more to live on, and I told Charlie so, but Mendenhall over-persuaded him. He solemnly promised him two things: First, that he would send a bateau with provisions in a few weeks; and then, at the end of three months, he would be sure to come himself, and take us away. So, very much against my will, we went to Isle Royale on the first of July. Having a bark canoe and a net, for a while we lived on fish, but one day about the end of summer a storm came, and we lost our canoe; and soon our net was broken, and good for nothing also. Oh, how we watched, and watched, and watched, but no bateau ever came to supply us with food; no vessel ever came to take us away; neither Mendenhall's nor any other. When at last we found that we had been deserted, and that we would have to spend the whole winter on the Island, and that there would be no getting away until spring, I tell you such a thought was hard to bear indeed. Our flour and butter and beans were gone. We couldn't catch any more fish. Nothing else seemed left to us but sickness, starvation, and death itself. All we could do was to eat bark, and roots and bitter berries that only seemed to make the hunger worse. Oh, sir, hunger is an awful thing. It eats you up so inside, and you feel so all gone, as if you must go crazy. If you could only see the holes I made around the cabin digging for something to eat, you would think it must have been some wild beast. O God, what I suffered there that winter from that terrible hunger, grace help me. I only wonder how I ever lived it through.

"Five days before Christmas (for you may be sure we kept account of every day) everything was gone. There was not so much as a single bean. The snow had come down thick, and heavy. It was bitter, bitter cold, and everything was frozen as hard as a stone. We hadn't any snow shoes. We couldn't dig any roots; we drew our belts tighter, and tighter; but it was no use; you can't cheat hunger; you can't fill up that inward craving that gnaws within you like a wolf.

"Charlie suffered from it even worse than I did. As he grew weaker, and weaker he lost all heart and courage. Then fever set in; it grew higher, and higher until at last he went clear out of his head. One day he sprang up, and seized his butcher knife, and began to sharpen it on a whetstone. He was tired of being hungry, he said, he would kill a sheep—something to eat he must have. And then, he glared at me as if he thought nobody could read his purpose but himself. I saw that I was the sheep he intended to kill and eat. All day, and all night long I watched him, and kept my eyes on him, not daring to sleep, and expecting him to spring upon me at any moment; but at last I managed to wrest the knife from him, and that danger was over. After the fever fits were gone, and he came to himself, he was as kind as ever; and I never thought of telling him what a dreadful thing he had tried to do. I tried hard not to have him see me cry as I sat behind him, but sometimes I could not help it, as I thought of our hard lot, and saw him sink away, and dry up until there was nothing left of him but skin and bones. At last he died so easily that I couldn't tell just when the breath did leave his body.

"This was another big trouble. Now that Charlie was dead, what could I do with him? I washed him, and laid him out but I had no coffin for him. How could I bury him when all around it was either rock or ground frozen as hard as a rock? And I could not bear to throw him out into the snow. For three days I remained with him in the hut, and it seemed almost like company to me, but I was afraid that if I continued to keep up the fire he would spoil. The only thing I could do was to leave him in the hut where I could sometimes see him, and go off and build a lodge for myself, and take my fire with me. Having sprained my arm in nursing and lifting Charlie, this was very hard work, but I did it at last.

"Oh, that fire, you don't know what company it was. It seemed alive just like a person with you, as if it could almost talk, and many a time, but for its bright and cheerful blaze that put some spirits in me, I think I would have just died. One time I made too big a fire and almost burned myself out, but I had plenty of snow handy, and so saved what I had built with so much labor, and took better care for the future.

"Then came another big trouble—ugh—what a trouble it was—the worst trouble of all. You ask me if I wasn't afraid when left alone on that island. Not of the things you speak of. Sometimes it would be so light in the north, and even away up overhead like a second sunset, that the night seemed turned into day; but I was used to the dancing spirits and was not afraid of them. I was not afraid of the Mackee Monedo or Bad Spirit, for I had been brought up better at the mission than to believe all the stories that the Indians told about him. I believed that there was a Christ, and that He would carry me through if

ILLUSTRATION BY STEPHEN D. VEIRS, JR.

I prayed to him. But the thing that most of all I was afraid of, and that I had to pray the hardest against was this: Sometimes I was so hungry, so very hungry, and the hunger raged so in my veins that I was tempted, Oh, how terribly was I tempted to take Charlie and make soup of him. I knew it was wrong, I felt it was wrong, I didn't want to do it, but some day the fever might come on me as it did on him, and when I came to my senses I might find myself in the very act of eating him up. Thank God, whatever else I suffered I was spared that; but I tell you of all the other things that was the thing of which I was the most afraid, and against which I prayed the most and fought the hardest.

"When the dreadful thought came over me, or I wished to die, and die quick, rather than suffer any longer, and I could do nothing else, then I would pray; and it always seemed to me after praying hard something would turn up, or I would think of something that I had not thought of before, and have new strength given me to fight it out still longer. One time in particular I remember, not long after Charlie's death, when things were at their very worst. For more than a week I had had nothing to eat but bark, and how I prayed that night that the good God would give me something to eat, lest the ever-increasing temptation would come over me at last. The next morning when I opened the door, I noticed for the first time some rabbit tracks. It almost took away my breath, and made my blood run through my veins like fire. In a moment I had torn a lock of hair out of my head, and was plaiting strands to make a snare for them. As I set it, I prayed that I might catch a fat one, and catch him quick. That very day I caught one, and so raging hungry was I that I tore off his skin and ate him up raw. It was nearly a week before I caught another, and so it was often for weeks together. The thing that seemed so very strange to me was though I had torn half the hair out of my head to make snares, never once during the whole winter did I catch two rabbits at one time.

"Oh, how heavily did the time hang upon me. It seemed as if the old moon would never wear out and the new one never come. At first I tried to sleep all that I could, but after a while I got into such a state of mind and body that I could scarcely get any sleep night or day. When I sat still for an hour or two, my limbs were so stiff and dried up that it was almost impossible for me to move them at all; so at last, like a bear in a cage, I found myself walking all the time. It was easier to walk than to do anything else. When I could do nothing else to relieve my hunger, I would take a pinch of salt. Early in March, I found a canoe that had been cast ashore, which I mended and made fit for use. Part of the sail I cut up, and made the strips into a net. Soon the little birds began to come, and then I knew that spring was coming in good earnest. God indeed had heard my prayer and I felt that I was saved. Once more I could see my mother.

"One morning in May, I had good luck fishing and caught no less than four mullets at one time. Just as I was cooking them for breakfast I heard a gun, and I fell back almost fainting. Then I heard another gun and I started to run down to the landing but my knees gave way, and I sank to the ground. Another gun—and I was off to the boat in time to meet the crew when they came ashore. The very first man that landed was Mendenhall, and he put up his hand to shake hands with me, which I did. 'Where is Charlie?' said he. I told him he was asleep. He might go up to the hut and see for himself. Then they all ran off together. When Mendenhall went into the hut, he saw that Charlie was dead. The men took off Charlie's clothes and shoes, and saw plain enough that I had not killed him, but that he had died of starvation. When I came up, Mendenhall began to cry and to try to explain things. He said that he had sent off a bateau with provisions, and didn't see why they didn't get to us. But the boys told me it was all a lie. I was too glad to get back to my mother to do anything. I thought his own conscience ought to punish him more than I could do."

• • • •

Angelique performed many remarkable feats of strength in after years. It is said that she once made a wager with a Frenchman that she could carry a barrel of pork to the top of a nearby hill and back. She won that wager with ease, and upon her return volunteered to carry the barrel up again with the Frenchman on top. Angelique lived to a ripe old age, dying at Sault Ste. Marie in 1874.

From: "A Biographical Sketch of the Lake Superior Iron Country" written by Ralph D. Williams and published in 1905 by the Penton Publishing Co., Cleveland.

Isle Royale Leisure

INTRODUCTION - *What started as an article on "resorts" turned into "recreation" and then widened further into "leisure." Leisure activities and the appreciation of the Island are crucial to consider since they were the spark that led to the protection of Isle Royale as a national park. Still, I had to be selective; there was too little room to discuss Island music and dance, the ever-present card games, special foods whose recipes are guarded family secrets, or photography. The following essay is only a prologue, and I invite everyone to ponder further why we, and those before us, have found so much enjoyment knowing the Island.*

Tim Cochrane, park historian

When early peoples came to Isle Royale they brought with them the human urge to find pleasure and artistry while on the Island. The historic Ojibwa invented many means of investing art and entertainment into their daily round of living. Canoes were made to be functional and pleasing to the eye. Between Sugar Mountain and Mount Desor, Ojibwa women poured boiling sugar maple sap in molds shaped like boreal forest animals and mythic creatures.[1] The same women made attractive moccasins out of [caribou?] hide to sell to copper miners at Island Mine.

European-American leisure-time pursuits began with "pleasure seekers" on excursion ships coming to Isle Royale as early as the 1860s. Northern elites traveled the lakes on large and well-appointed steamers and schooners like the *Ironsides*, whose crew offered brass and string bands.[2] Other ships championed "sumptuous meals," perhaps as a safe and novel repast from the crushing news of the Civil War. Ships such as the *Keweenaw*, the propeller *Michigan*, *Pewabic*, *Norman*, *City of Toledo*, *Union*, and the *Manistee* brought well-heeled visitors from Cleveland, Detroit, and the Superior south shore to Isle Royale. Feverish

85

mining activity at Silver Islet outside of Thunder Bay and the construction of the Canadian Pacific Railroad meant dozens of boats were criss-crossing Lake Superior in the 1870s. They also would stop at Island and Minong mines' wharfs. These early visits were typically short, like those made by the passengers on the *City of Cleveland*, "who were boated over to Rock Harbor for the afternoon to pick greenstones."[3] Others fished for trout. Most of the cruise "amusements" were centered on deck, however, and the Island visits added a romantic flair to a lake voyage. Fleeting views of the jagged shoreline from the comfortable deck was a forerunner leisure-time activity on the Island.

A growing national pride in American "scenery" and landscapes led people to Isle Royale in the last decades of the 1800s. A Duluth-based "Isle Royale Club" camped at the head of Siskitwit Bay and each evening built roaring bonfires. Fishing parties also tented at the abandoned Rock Harbor Lighthouse and at small islands. Interest in aesthetics and the sporting life of camping compelled "four artists from Duluth . . . [to take] views of the Island" in 1889.[4] Despite the growing interest in the rugged life, only hardy brook trout fishermen ventured into the Island's interior. Most excursioneers remained confined to accessible shoreline and boat access. The steam yacht *Picket* was a frequent visitor to Isle Royale in the 1890s and brought many anglers to fish for brook trout in the Big and Little Siskiwit rivers, the Siskiwit Lake outlet, and Washington Creek. By 1900, Isle Royale became the object of many well-to-do people's recreational desires. For the first time, middle-class Americans had the time and disposable income for vacationing on Isle Royale.

Yet the Island was also the place for more native and homespun types of recreation. People working and living on the Island picked greenstones and berries, trolled, and caught four-to-five-pound "monster" speckled trout in Conglomerate Bay.[5] The Menagerie Island Lighthouse keepers, for example, made regular "speckled trout" fishing trips to the Siskiwit Lake "outlet" and Hay Bay, and on one occasion live caught 36 brookies to "treat" the lighthouse inspector. The Light keepers also "picked some wild flowers," and shot black ducks, "plovers," and "prairie chickens." U.S. Lake Surveyors and mine officials held gentlemanly "shoots" of passenger pigeons.[6] Generally of much more modest means, miners' and lighthouse keepers' recreation was more dependent upon Isle Royale resources. Greenstoning remained a favorite, the Light keepers removing kegs of greenstone gravel to sift through during the lull times.[7]

More and more people sought to relax, fish, and "take views" on Isle Royale in the late 1890s. Boat service to the Island became much more regular, permitting freer access to Island locations. A. Booth and Company boats—the *Camp*, then the *Hiram R. Dixon*, and finally the beloved *America*—brought regular passenger, mail, and freight service to Isle Royale residents. Still, would-be recreationists were handicapped by the lack of facilities. The Johns family, lead by patriarch John F. Johns and his sons Willie and Edgar, solved this problem by opening Isle Royale's first hotel in 1892. The "Johns Hotel" evolved from providing a spare room to lingering ship passengers, to catering to paying guests. Despite rudimentary accommodations, the hotel business flourished and the Johnses responded by building five log cottages and a second story to their "hall." John Johns and his sons built the hall out of tamarack logs cut in two nearby bogs and hauled to the site by two Newfoundland dogs. Two organs were then added to the hall. Guests lodged in the upstairs rooms of the hall or in tiny cottages, the smallest being 6 feet by 8 feet. Like many other Island resort operators to follow, the Johnses responded to the "good times" by constructing a few more tourist cabins around the grounds. A white picket fence divided paying guests from the Johnses' commitment to self-reliance— cows, chickens, sheep, and pigs for food production. Restricted by a lack of capital and luxurious accommodations, the Johnses sold their pioneering hotel and island to George Barnum in 1902. The Johnses continued to live on the island, fish commercially, and ironically opened the "Johns Post Office"—a symbol of settlement and community stability—after their hotel had closed.

Another Island family, the Mattsons of Tobin Harbor, determined to im-prove their meager livelihood on Isle Royale by operating a resort. Gust Mattson opened his small, homespun Tobin Habor Summer Resort on Minong Island in part because "his wife was a good cook, and more and more people started coming."[8] Mattson's place gained a following of guests from Duluth, who returned frequently. Again handicapped by few assets, Mattson could not compete with the more luxurious resorts opening at Washington Island and Rock Harbor. He sold his resort and along with his sons quietly resumed com-mercial fishing.

Island fisherman, Erick Johnson, shared Gust Mattson's dream of a better life by establishing a resort at his fishery in Rock Harbor. Johnson, an ambi-tious Swede-Finn, established Tourist Home Resort at Davidson Island in 1902. Like many fishermen, Johnson was a self-reliant individual who brought all his talents to the resort operation. When not fishing, Johnson built frame and log buildings and boats at what would later be named Davidson Island. Guests were treated to Mrs. Johnson's renowned fried fish, and passed time by greenstoning and hiking, and with sing-a-longs at night.[9] In a Tourist Home brochure, guests were also encouraged to watch a "Finlander's" fishing operation. The same brochure appealed to guests to reconsider a lake cruise and stay at Tourist Home instead of a trip to Europe. And, no doubt, A. Booth and Company were happy to be compared in the same light as the trans-Atlantic trade advertised in Tourist Home's promotional materials. It certainly was a much better deal: Guests could stay at Tourist Home for $1.75 a day or $10.00 a week.[10] Johnson's promotional deal with A. Booth and Company obligated him to build a big dock so that Booth vessels could safely and conveniently moor at his resort. His string of small cabins huddled around the end of the big dock. Despite Johnson's and Booth's best efforts, interest in Tourist Home was eclipsed by more elegant and commodious Isle Royale resorts. Making the most of his labors, Johnson sold the place to the Davidson family and a number of his buildings to the newly christened Minong Island Resort in Tobin Harbor (formerly Gust Mattson's resort).

At the opening of the twentieth century, Island recreationists could find simple accommodations, with little creature comforts or elegance, in Washington, Tobin, and Rock harbors. An awkward relationship arose between early Island recreationists—often Victorian elites in stiff collars—with pioneering resorts and their hardscrabble owners. One of the regular "bigshots" to Isle Royale was Colonel C. H. Graves of Duluth. A celebrated veteran of the Civil War, founder of the Duluth Board of Trade (a shipping cartel), and later ambassador to Sweden, Graves was a devoted speckled trout fisherman. He solved, in part, the lodging problem by purchasing the 84-foot, 39-ton steam yacht *Picket*. He fished North Shore streams and later moved his attention and heart to catching Isle Royale brookies.

Along with his business colleague, Marshall H. Alworth, Graves spearheaded efforts to establish the Washington Harbor Club, an exclusive club of Duluth elites fond of fishing and the rarified atmosphere of an all-male society. In 1902 the Washington Club was formed with twenty Duluthians contributing $300 for membership to purchase buildings left over from the Wendigo Mining Company at the head of Washington Harbor. At the club, steel company executives, shipping magnates, and other powerful men fished, were catered to by servants, and informally arranged grand business deals. Members held exclusive fishing rights to Washington and Grace creeks until 1938, when the club was disbanded and its holdings purchased by the National Park Commission. Club members took stream fishing seriously; they even erected a small cabin at the mouth of Washington Harbor to guard against fishing trespass.

Early fisherman in Isle Royale's backcountry.

Club members were influential and well-off, but others with only slightly less monetary resources began coming to the Island at the same time. Vacationers were increasingly drawn to Isle Royale because of its reputation as a haven from hay fever and Midwestern heat. The influence of Lake Superior makes "Isle Royale air" cool, soothing, and moist—the perfect relief from dry, pollen-laden air of the Midwest. Kneut Kneutson was one such refugee from hay fever who also saw the logic of starting an Island resort. After greenstoning, while sailing back to his lodging at the Gust Mattson fishery and resort in Tobin Harbor, he serendipitously discovered Snug Harbor and immediately realized its advantageous location. He quickly bought a mile of frontage, platted out streets and house lots, and built Park Place, a resort which later became the Rock Harbor Lodge.[11] Kneutson and a partner, John E. Tappen, invested in

Park Place, and quickly a row of cabins flanking Snug Harbor sprung up. One of these cabins, the Spruces, remains on the Rock Harbor waterfront, while another, the Jack cabin [of the Ace, King, Queen, Jack string] has been relocated to Bangsund Cabin in the Rock Harbor channel.

After a few years of directing a flourishing establishment, Commodore Kneutson's attention focused on the mainland and Park Place languished. His mainland real estate business which provided Kneutson the capital to open Park Place now drew him away. But Kneutson's example sparked others' interest in developing fine resorts. A growing group of entrepreneurs became interested in establishing Island resorts, especially since A. Booth and Company promoted them and ran the reliable and spacious *Dixon* on the North Shore–Isle Royale run. Booth held a monopoly on Island trade (fish, freight, and passenger) until Captain Singer of the Lake Michigan & Lake Superior Transportation Company sought to break Booth's grip on Lake Superior trade.

Captain Singer sought to challenge Booth on the water and on land. He purchased the *Bon Ami* and later the sleek, quick, 200-passenger vessel *Iroquois* for the North Shore–Isle Royale trade. Booth responded by placing the fast and relatively luxurious *America* on the same route, competing bow-to-bow with Singer's *Iroquois*. In 1902, the grandiose nature of Singer's challenge was unveiled. Workmen labored on "Singerville," with floating docks, water tower, ten cottages (each with a satellite outhouse), ice house, barn, main building, and a pavilion. A couple of his cottages remain standing today, now occupied by Sivertson family members. Singer called his resort Island House, and he meant it. The main building was almost 150 feet long, and included 22 bedrooms, a barber shop, lobby, pool room, and expansive porches with views of the harbor and of the Ontario and Minnesota shoreline.[12] But it was the pavilion that caused the most stir. Singer's pavilion was a combination dance hall and bowling alley. In 1910 he added a wireless radio tower on Sunset Rock to communicate with vessels about weather and sea conditions and make guest reservations. The entire complex was said to have cost Captain Singer $80,000. And for help to meet the exigencies of running an Island resort, Singer hired Island-wise John Johns, the founder of the resort business on Isle Royale.[13]

From its opening until 1920, Island House was the class of Island resorts. It began the golden era of resorts on Isle Royale. Its amenities, dances, bowling, and opulent style attracted guests. Easy access by elegant ships with rail connections to midwestern cities brought guests from Chicago, Detroit, Milwaukee, or the Twin Cities to the Island House. In fact, enough people came to Singerville from the North Shore–Isle Royale route through Port Arthur Ontario, that a customs house was established on the grounds. While Singerville thrived, Singer's watery empire was sinking. His workhorse vessel, *Bon Ami*, burned to the water line. Frequent navigational errors plagued the *Iroquois* as she ran into docks and other vessels. Pestered by lawsuits and the undiminished competition from A. Booth Company, Captain Singer's vessels were forced from the lake trade. Reportedly, Singer drowned a few years later.

Across the harbor, but in full view of the Island House, was perhaps the most humble type of lodging establishment run during the modern era. More of a boarding house than a resort, the Saul family opened a lodging place on Booth Island for immigrant fishermen working for A. Booth and Company. Housed in a two-story, eight-room house, Norwegian-American fishermen toiled to be free of their indenture to Booth fisheries. Tragically, Saul contracted tuberculosis, sold his boarding house, and built a native stone house on Long Point, complete with a battery of windows for sunning himself.

Salesman Fred Schofield began a new, classy resort on what had been called Fish Island on the northeast end of Isle Royale. Schofield was ambitious, and he purchased all of Fish Island and surrounding satellite islands. He then peddled the surrounding islands to long-term guests and associates. With the instincts of a salesman, he immediately renamed the island Belle Isle, a more illustrious name. Schofield was determined to challenge all other resorts on Isle Royale and he had one great advantage—location. The mainstay of Island passenger vessels, those running the North Shore route, stopped first at Belle Isle after leaving Fort William/Port Arthur. Thus, *America* passengers would first spot the symbol of Belle Isle Resort: a wigwam perched up to be seen (and not lived in—it had a cement floor). Further, at first landfall, passengers would see the Belle Resort buildings and grounds in its entirety. Schofield was not about to let his geographic advantage slip by. He and his staff would actively solicit passengers destined for other resorts to disembark at what he acclaimed as the grandest of all Isle Royale resorts.

Belle Isle was a graceful and upscale resort for the times. The main lodge overlooked Belle Harbor and was appointed with a fieldstone fireplace, oriental rugs, and pine panelling. Eventually, Belle Isle had 28 cottages and two central bath houses with electricity. But it was Schofield's commitment to novel entertainment which surpassed his competition by far. Schofield imported recreational types uncharacteristic of the Island. He put up tennis and shuffleboard courts, and bettered Isle Royale geography by walling in a swimming pool. Workers created the swimming pool by cutting off an alcove of Lake Superior with a cement wall. Sheltered from most winds and warmed by the sun a few hardy guests could take to the water. Schofield also took a notion to add a golf course to his resort. After blasting rock and hauling in soil from McCargoe Cove, the Belle Isle short course was born and in operation. Because of Schofield's dream, campers at the present-day campground enjoy sweeping vistas of the harbor from the old golf grounds. Schofield added all these mainland sporting opportunities to the usual Island pastimes: rock hounding, moose watching at salt licks, and trolling. Employees would frequently take out large trolling parties on a big scow for $1.00 apiece.

Belle Isle and virtually all other Island resorts both relied upon and benefited commercial fishermen. A symbiotic relationship began. Herman Johnson and his partner John Anderson sold fish regularly to the Belle Isle Resort.

Trolling for lake trout was a popular sport.

Arnold and Milford Johnson and Pete Edisen served as resort guides and later ran their own boat concession at Rock Harbor, Belle Isle, and Windigo. Fishermen served as caretakers, boat and dock builders, mechanics, operators of resort boats, and "entertainers." Fishermen provided a distinctive character to Isle Royale that entranced many resort visitors and made their stay memorable. Some, like the Indian fisherman-guide John Linklater at Birch Island, became an Island institution. Rock Harbor Lodge had regular summer trips to McCargoe Cove so guests could be enthralled by Linklater's campfire stories, Indian heritage, woods-wisdom, and quiet ways.

Competition among resort owners heated up in the '20s. Both the Tobin Harbor Lodge and the Rock Harbor Lodge responded to Schofield's challenge and made vast improvements. Still, each resort had a character of its own. Mother-daughter proprietresses, Mrs. Helen Smith and Helena Smith Arborgust, of Tobin Harbor, created a family atmosphere at their retreat. Known for Mrs. Smith's famous pies, often from the famed rhubarb patch at Passage Island, Tobin's attracted an older crowd. One doctor arriving at the lodge queried Mrs. Smith, "Do you have phones?" She sheepishly responded, "No." The doctor brightened and said, "Good, then I'll stay longer."[14] Guests enjoyed small cottages in a wooded glade, evening talks, and dancing to the resort's Victrola. Mrs. Smith raised a garden for fresh greens. Boat tours to the Passage Island Light Station also were a favorite. To meet other needs of her guests, Mrs. Smith frequently arranged for Sunday church services.

By 1920, Kneutson's Park Place was sputtering along under the Commodore's good intentions, but split attention. Kneutson realized he could not run a profitable and progressive resort from a distance. His business acumen told him that Island resorts were most successful if they had a distinctive character and personable management. To solve these problems and his emotional commitment to Park Place, he passed management of the lodge to his daughter, Mrs. Bertha Farmer. With a renewed family commitment to the resort and a new name, the Rock Harbor Lodge, Mrs. Farmer set about modernizing and expanding the resort. First to be built was the two story Guest House that sits prominently overlooking the Rock Harbor channel. The Guest House became both the primary lodging facility and a symbol of the renovated resort. Electric lights, hot water, and the coming of indoor flush toilets to Isle Royale added a new level of creature comforts to overnighting at the Island. The Rock Harbor Lodge quickly became a more fashionable resort.

Mrs. Farmer's personable management of the resurrected Rock Harbor

Lodge attracted a new wave of loyal guests. Her lodge was rustic, with a birch-bark sign on the Guest House to match the birchbark napkin rings with each guest's name on it. A younger crowd could enjoy croquet or a tennis lesson taught by Coach Orsborn, or go on berry or greenstone "picking" expeditions, while an older Commodore Kneutson lent a hand to the operation, chatting and storytelling with guests. Another Kneutson idea, lodge boats towing strings of dories full of fishermen, became a hallmark activity of the lodge. These strings of dory fishermen trolled for lake trout up and down the Rock Harbor channel. Mrs. Farmer sought to establish a genteel atmosphere in which employees were supposed to only speak to guests when spoken to. Mrs. Farmer's astute management and emotional commitment helped keep the lodge in business during the Depression years. As fewer and fewer guests came, it became expedient to run an efficient operation with a good reputation to keep guests coming back.

Tobin Harbor Lodge and Rock Harbor Lodge had an advantage that other resorts lacked, in that they were surrounded by flourishing summer colonies. In Tobin Harbor particularly, summer cottagers created a sense of activity, community life, and customs that drew in resort guests. Oftentimes guests were friends or acquaintances of the Tobin Harbor summer people. Resort guests learned to enjoy harbor customs, such as Tobin Harbor residents hurrying to raise their flags each morning. Lodge operators encouraged intermingling with summer people who knew and actively appreciated the Island, and who raised lodge guests' admiration for the archipelago and "their harbor."

A number of summer cottagers lived in the immediate vicinity of the Rock Harbor Lodge and participated in some lodge affairs. However, the summer community at Rock Harbor was smaller than at Tobin. Still, the members of the Langworthy, Warren, Ralph, and Orsborn families participated in the resort's croquet matches and annual tennis tournament. Other summer people with cottages scattered around Isle Royale made use of resorts such as Belle Isle, the Island House, and even the Washington Club. Often from the same home towns and socioeconomic milieu, there was frequent mixing between resort guests and the Island's summer people.

The 1930s were tough years for Isle Royale resorts. The Great Depression meant fewer guests and the shipwreck of the *America* in 1928 crimped easy and comfortable access to resorts until the *Winyah* began the Isle Royale route. Despite these drawbacks, Holger and Lucy Johnson opened the Johnson's Resort and Trading Post in Chippewa Harbor during the Depression years. Searching

Sitting fireside at the lodge

for new ways to support his family, Holger added the resort to his commercial fishery, fur trapping, and informal business of polishing and selling greenstones. He also opened the trading post to furnish goods, some supplies, and hand-made birchbark souvenirs to boaters voyaging around the Island. Holger Johnson's eldest daughter, Violet Miller, remembers being the shop keeper at the post when a boat arrived:

> They could hear the boats coming from a long way away. They got so they could tell what boat it was. Somehow, the psychology of it, if you went there and opened the door just as they got off their boat, they'd rush right in.[15]

The Johnson's Resort was for guests who would like to "rough it." Indeed, the Johnson's stressed outdoor entertainment, especially fishing, hiking, moose watching, greenstoning, and some craft work. The Johnson's had informal portages/moose trails to lakes Whittlesey, Richie, and Mason, and had boats stashed at these lakes for their enthusiastic guests. Guests stayed in the seven freshly-hewn log cabins and ate with the Johnson family in the main residence at Chippewa Harbor. Guests who enjoyed outdoor activities, simple accommodations, and participation with a family who intimately knew the

Island were happy. If Holger thought his guests found the accommodations wanting, he freely offered to boat them up to the Rock Harbor Lodge. Since the Johnsons were one of a handful of families that regularly overwintered on the Island, guests queried family members, "What was it like during isolated winters?" Besides enjoying nature, guests were treated to music provided by Holger and his oldest daughters and sons. Keeping his operation small and run entirely by family members kept the resort and trading post in operation, despite the Depression. The outdoor recreational activities on which the Johnson family hung the success of their business were a precursor to today's recreational pursuits.

By the late '30s, it was the movement to establish Isle Royale National Park that closed Johnson's and, after a period of adjustment, other resorts around Isle Royale, except for Rock Harbor Lodge. The resort era on Isle Royale was coming to a close. And with it the closings of "exotic" or "imported" forms of recreation such as tennis, croquet, and golf. The passing of the resort era meant the passing of strong personalities in the resort trade. Mrs. Smith of Tobin Lodge sold out to the National Park Commission. The Singer estate also was happy to sell out, recouping some money from resort buildings and grounds that had gone to seed. Other changes were afoot, as the movement to establish Isle Royale gained momentum. Bertha Farmer and Fred Schofield began to wonder how they might, or might not, benefit from an Island park. Transportation to the Island was in flux. Ships running regular service to the Island became less attractive and romantic. Sporadic airplane service to the Island began in the 1930s with the Royale Line's two-propeller amphibious plane and Dusty Rhodes' seaplane, *Spirit of St. Louis County* [Minnesota]. Biological tumult also caused problems as the 1936 fire scorched one-fifth of the Island and a moose die-off created an unglamorous atmosphere. For example, Mrs. Smith's employees remember having to haul off a winter's toll of foul-smelling rotten moose carcasses.

Fred Schofield and Bertha Farmer found the ground rules for operating a lodge after the park was created had been changed. Once proud owners of their establishments, they sold their places, and now operated them through a contract with the Park Service. Clashes in values ensued. The tradition of resorts with a strong "personality" and individuality clashed with National Park Service drives towards standardization. Fred Schofield tried to stay on and run Belle Isle, but cancer soon forced him to quit. Mrs. Farmer was then charged to run Rock Harbor Lodge, Belle Isle, and Windigo Inn—occupying buildings left over from the Washington Harbor Club. But Mrs. Farmer's primary attention was captured by "her" establishment in Rock Harbor. Belle Isle Resort closed in 1946, and Windigo Inn quietly closed in 1973.

The establishment of Isle Royale National Park highlights a new, emerging sense of aesthetics toward the archipelago. The struggle toward establishing the park forced people to articulate what Isle Royale meant and should be. For the summer cottagers and long-time resort guests, the change in ownership heightened a sense of history and a sense of belonging to the Island. The creation of the park awakened a national audience to the benefits and resources of Isle Royale. Appreciating Isle Royale was thereafter put in a national context; its relatively pristine environs heightened by the bustle and soot of urban life. It became a wilderness in the eyes of many because it stood out from places of regular commerce, industry, and dwelling. National Park Service management meant the Island was managed for the first time as a whole, not as distinctive harbors or individualized resorts. Recreational pursuits on the Island changed, mirroring societal changes. The resort tradition continued but "exotic" sporting activities, like golfing and tennis, were the first to go. Visitors sought out Isle Royale more as a retreat than as a recreational spa.

This change in what people came to Isle Royale for did not occur overnight, nor was it without its upheavals. Visitation to the Island climbed after World War II, but many of the visitors were passengers on the big cruise boats *South American*, *Alabama*, and *North American*. Port of call at Isle Royale for these boats was only a few, but very hectic, hours. By the 1950s, visitation was at a low ebb, in the days before many Americans' concern for the natural environment. However, more and more area residents could afford private boats and more boaters made a trip over to the Island to fish, vacation with friends, and visit with commercial fishermen.

The "ecological movement" born in the 1960s and continuing today, created, in effect, a backpacking era on Isle Royale. Visitation sharply climbed after the Island was featured in national magazines. The Park Service responded by opening new trails, such as the Minong Ridge Trail, and by completing the Feldtmann Loop. The "invention" of American interest in wildlands and ecological consciousness, and American affluence, made Isle Royale attractive to more people. The age of Island visitors dropped (compared with the resort era) as its natural charms and vigors of outdoor recreation were in the spotlight. The National Park Service responded by building new facilities, docks, campgrounds, and trails to meet this growing and changing demand.

Leisure and the pursuit of pleasure on the archipelago is as old as man's inhabitation of Isle Royale—over 3,500 years old. Anglo-American recreation is at least 130 years old, and continues today as the principal use of Isle Royale. Through the last 130 years, recreational pursuits have slowly pushed from the shoreline into the interior. A shipboard "view" of the Island has changed to backpackers discovering the secrets and enchantment of the interior. The rustic resorts have closed and Rock Harbor Lodge has been drastically altered. Hunting ceased in 1925. Still, the tradition of resorts catering to guests continues, though in a much modified form. Rangers now guide guests where resort employees and fishermen had in the past. Today's formalized "walks" and evening programs take the place of informal chats with a knowledgeable Island enthusiast. The glorious era of stalking the wily brook trout has been eclipsed by boaters with elaborate downriggers trolling for lake trout. Still, a core of recreational traditions persist and all are based on Island resources—greenstoning, fishing, moose watching, birding, appreciating forests and water, storytelling, and exploring evidence of human settlement on the captivating archipelago.

1. Mrs. Henry Conary, "Early Life on Isle Royale," *Daily Mining Gazette*, 21 June 1939.

2. *Portage Lake Mining Gazette*, 8 July 1865.

3. *Portage Lake Mining Gazette*, 26 July 1862.

4. Menagerie Lighthouse Log, 5 August 1889.

5. Emmet Hoyt Scott Papers, "Diary," 18 August 1876, and "Scott Autobiography," Lilly Library, Indiana University.

6. U.S. Lake Surveyors Notes, 1867 and 1868, Cheynoweth Collection, Copper Country Archives, Michigan Technological University.

7. Menagerie Lighthouse Log, 8–14 July 1886 and 24 July 1889, Mott Island Archive, Isle Royale National Park.

8. Oral history interview with Reuben Hill, January 18, 1984, Larsmont, Minnesota, interviewed by Carol Maass. Oral History Collection, Isle Royale National Park.

9. Interview with Mrs. Gordon Hendrickson, July 6, 1984, interviewed by Carol Maass. Oral History Collection, Isle Royale National Park.

10. Tourist Home Resort brochure, Mott Island Archives, Isle Royale National Park.

11. Kneut Kneutson, "Memoirs of a Pioneer," Undated manuscript, Mott Island Archive, Isle Royale National Park.

12. Singer Resort Building file, Mott Island Archives, Isle Royale National Park.

13. Interview with Edgar Johns, September, 1965, interviewed by Lawrence Rakestraw. Oral History Collection, Isle Royale National Park.

14. Rueben Hill interview, January 18, 1984.

15. Interview with Violet Miller, October 2, 1986, Ahmeek, Michigan, interviewed by Tim Cochrane. Oral History Collection, Isle Royale National Park.